HOW TO BECOME A SUCCESSFUL IMMIGRANT

9 Ways to Turn Your Struggle Into Success

LINDA SALAS

Award Winning Author

10-10-10 Publishing

HOW TO BECOME A SUCCESSFUL IMMIGRANT:
9 Ways to Turn Your Struggle Into Success.

Published by:
10-10-10- Publishing
Markham, Ontario

Copyright © 2017 by Linda Salas

First 10-10-10 publishing paperback edition February 2017 Second 10-10-10 Publishing paperback edition February 2017.

Salas, Linda.

HOW TO BECOME A SUCCESSFUL IMMIGRANT
9 Ways to Turn Your Struggle into Success

ISBN: 978-1-77277-126-8

I dedicate this book to every youth, adult, elder and every person that is open to change, challenges, and stepping forward into fear; it does not matter what language you speak, what your religion is, or what cultural beliefs you hold; it is time for you to tap into a life of ABUNDANCE.

TABLE OF CONTENTS

FOREWORD

D EAR READER....
Are you living the life of ABUNDANCE you wish to have? Are you the author of your own life? Do you wish to travel to another country or immigrate, but you feel so frozen by fear that you haven't made that leap?

Do you feel empty and wish to live a life of ABUNDANCE?

Would you like to discover your mission on this planet and do it while you become wealthier, happier, healthier and tap into ABUNDANCE?

Would you like to learn more about a multicultural country outside of your home country? If you are considering moving to a new place, you need to know how to overcome various challenges, including a language barrier, but there is so much more to be considered!

No matter who you are or what your current situation is, regardless of your age, culture, beliefs or religion, this book is full of insights and will act as a guide in your life, advising you on the steps to take before you move, and teach you how to fulfill your purpose once you have made the move to a new country.

Linda Salas was an immigrant herself, moving from Mexico to Canada, coming from a small town named San Juan del Rio,

Queretaro. After making the decision to change her life and the lives of future generations, she moved to Canada, despite not knowing one word of English. Linda is now the CEO of her company, LSF Immigration Consulting, and she is a true example of what you can become when you apply everything Linda teaches you within this book.

From her own experiences immigrating, as well as the experience she has gained in her 11 years of assisting others to immigrate, Linda has written *How to Become a Successful Immigrant* so that you can turn your struggle into success, just as she did.

Linda shares with you all her personal experiences to help you to overcome fear and move to the place you wish to live. She believes that where you were born is not in your hands, but where you end your life is your decision and responsibility. This guide will help you to settle in the country you are immigrating to, will guide you in how to upgrade your education, become an entrepreneur, and manage your time and your money.

If you require any immigration or legal advice, Linda Salas and the company she represents is definitely the place for you to go and become successful. Get ready to read this amazing journey and get ready to create a massive change in your life, finances, and tap into ABUNDANCE.

—**Raymond Aaron**
New York Times Bestselling Author

ACKNOWLEDGMENTS

I WOULD FIRST LIKE TO THANK my husband, Stephen Fraser, for the support he has provided me from the first day we began our joint journey through this life. My mission would not be complete without his tremendous support, allowing me to dream big, and always believing in me and my BIG DREAMS. I could not be more blessed than when I am beside you.

I would like to give all my recognition to my beautiful daughters, Makayla and Katherine Salas-Fraser; for all the support that you provided me at your young age, for choosing me in this journey to be your mother. You chose a busy mother, but you were ready to support her. Even though we are not together when mama has to travel, you are always in my heart.

I would like to thank my parents, Felipe Salas and Antonia Perez, for all the love you gave me, because that was all you had. You could not give something you didn't have and I became aware of this at a very young age in my life, and because of that, my love and compassion grew for you.

I would like to thank my siblings, especially Felipe Salas, for all those childhood memories that we shared in life and for those difficult times but strong bonds. I recognize the great human being you are. I love you from the deepest part of my heart. To my other two young brothers; Salvador Salas, for the beauty you show, not only from the outside but the inside, and for always bringing your negotiation skills. Even when others want to fight, you always want peace. Thank you for choosing to become a lawyer, such a humble profession where knowledge of the law and helping others is your mission. Marco Salas, for the big talents I know you have. Even though you haven't discovered them yet, you will find your way I am sure. Last but not least, my beautiful sister BELEN SALAS, the only sister with a 20-year age difference, but you carry the old soul of a 40-year-old human. What an intuition, an ability to live and enjoy life, what intelligence and character, and what confidence you have! Congratulations for being so strong and a light for so many humans. I love you from the depths of my heart.

To my mentors and teachers from preschool all the way to my Bachelor's and Master's Degrees, to all of you for your dedication to teach and show me the ways you knew. A special thanks to my professional mentors, Michael Golden and Max Wolpert.

I would like to thank my dear friend and spiritual sister, Alaide Santacruz, for her tremendous support by reading this book and giving me her invaluable comments, editing it, and also for encouraging me to believe more in the value in it.

To my mentors, who have helped me to be who I am today in a such a short period of time, Harv Ecker, Robert Kiyosaki, Bob Proctor, Raymond Aaron, Michael Silver, and the coaches that have been close to me and helped me to achieve the highest version of myself.

Thank you to my current team, Antonio Sousa, Lucy Nguyen, Salvador Salas, and Itzel Diaz, for all your support and thank you for giving the best of yourselves each day to provide the best service to others.

INTRODUCTION

W HAT IF THERE WAS A GPS where you could enter a code to receive instructions for the best way to immigrate to another western country, and the best way to successfully settle in that country? Do you think this would be helpful? I think so, because this would help you to find your way even faster than I did.

I will share my experience and knowledge with you, and give you the valuable information of what I did to be a successful immigrant in Canada. I think you can do it in 5 years, even 2 years, if you continue reading this book.

I come from two countries; one that is a rich country culturally and economically and the other one that is poor in the same two ways. In one country, I was born and raised and the other one I chose.

For my first twenty-five years, I lived in my birth country. I completed a Bachelor's Degree in Law. I was raised by a middle-class family, although my father barely completed secondary school and my mother hardly knows how to write. However, regardless of their academic condition, they managed a business and created a fair amount of wealth.

Once I reached the age of 21, I was employed by the government. While still attending law school, I managed to get into politics and become part of the government. I was in the area of Human Resources, where I managed the hiring and firing process for the government. I saw many people who were afraid every time they learned a government change was coming. I saw the fear in a lot of people. I saw people that after working for many years were fired without any justifications. The longer I worked there, the more money I made, but I was not happy because of the system. I knew there must be another way; that people should not live in fear of government change.

I asked myself why the government would just fire and hire whoever they wanted and do it with our money, the money of the citizens who reside there and pay taxes. However, no matter how much I argued with my boss that it was not right to fire someone like that, he always replied, "There is nothing we can do. Just do your part and enjoy your salary and benefits while they last." I could not believe I would live this way all my life. I didn't have many options at that time because I needed to complete my degree, which was my goal. I was also sure I did not want to have this same job, as my parents did, for many years.

After I completed my degree in 2005 I decided to travel since this was something that had been a dream of mine.

My friends were talking about a trip to Europe, so I decided to go along with them. I needed to experience what was outside my country. We travelled around England, France, Belgium and Spain. This trip alone helped me to see that there were other countries with different perspectives. The city that impacted and changed my life the most was Paris. This has nothing to do with the city, which is actually very pretty, but it had more to do with the cultural aspects. While riding the train, I saw everyone holding a book and reading. People seemed entertained by books. I spent a great deal of time observing the people in Paris, and I saw ladies in their suits riding on bikes. I am sure there were also men, but I paid more attention to the women.

I then noticed people happily talking on their phones in a coffee shop, or working on the street with their computers. A lot of people who were citizens were enjoying life during the afternoon. I realized these people must do something different than my country, because we work from sunrise until sunset. We could work for over 12 hours per day. We were exhausted and afraid of losing our jobs. We barely rode a bike and we were never able to sit and enjoy the sun during the day. We even had to work Saturdays, and if we were lucky, we would have Sunday off. Of course, this was not the case for my professional life, because I was one of the lucky ones who got a job at the government, but most of the middle class and lower class in my country were living this miserable life.

After finishing my trip, I was physically exhausted because of so much travelling, walking, and not eating and sleeping properly. There was so much to see and so little time to sleep. On the other side, I was excited because I now knew there was a place where things were different. I then travelled back to my town and sold my car right away. I was lucky that I had paid it off, because I worked and saved my money. Then I moved forward with my life change. I was determined to live a different life, to live the Paris life. I visited the library, read lots of personal development books, and began walking. I started running to my work instead of driving, because my town was not safe for bike riding, so I took the safer route of running. I would not fire any more people when it was unjustified. I fought with my bosses, managers and directors, but sometimes I could not win the battle. Sometimes I was only able to help them to transfer the employee from one place to another, instead of firing them.

I began visualizing a different life. I knew I needed to learn English to be able to study and graduate with a PhD in my country. This way, I might be able get transferred to work on a sociological research project in one of the countries that made its citizens happy versus a country whose citizens are living with being overworked, not to mention the low salaries. I began planning my trip to a country where I could learn English. I did not speak one word, but I was determined to learn a second language. What better language than English, which according to my reading and research was the business language of the world. I sold my car and my computer, then I quit my job. Those funds gave me a fair amount of money to go and make my dream happen. I pulled all my savings together and managed to come to my second country, Canada, which later become my adoptive country.

I could not learn the language as fast as I had planned on my road map. I did eventually learn, but more importantly, I was now living in a country offering better quality of life, better wages according to the services you offered, and in which a person can live happily and comfortably, even if they are just working selling coffee. I learned about the diversity of cultures. Most importantly, I could now use my profession to help others immigrate. I would say that in my decade of experience, I have helped thousands of immigrants to come and enjoy the rich cultural and economic benefits of my adoptive country.

I know you must be wondering about what my family and close friends thought about my decision to move to another country. I received a lot of negativity and very little support from the people close to me, who were surprised that I was leaving a desirable career with a good salary. Many people in my country were unable to get a job like this, and I was willing to leave it behind. My parents were a bit scared, but I explained to them that leaving was better for my future education. I needed to leave to learn English, but that this was to be a temporary move and then I would come back to further my education. My parents did believe strongly in education, so they would do anything they could to support my dream. I believed in education at that time, even though my perspective has changed since then. If you haven't finished your education or are one who revels at school, then keep reading this book and it will certainly help you to change your paradigm about education.

One obstacle many people who consider immigrating are concerned about is bringing family; be it a spouse, parent, or children. A family can immigrate all together at once, or one family member can go first to find a place to live and schools, with the rest of the family coming a few months later. I have helped a lot of immigrants to settle, and I know what is like to have a family that you have to move.

If you happen to be a young person who lives with your parents, and they are paying for your education, then you could be steps ahead because of the support and the family on your side. Just by living the experiences of a different culture and country, you can open the door to many opportunities in your life and create changes to your own perspective on life. All you may need to succeed is to travel abroad once.

Handling the emotions that come when you make a big decision as moving to another country requires work. You will feel quite emotional when you are in a different country. After you change from being a tourist to living permanently in this new country, either temporarily as a student, worker or as a new immigrant, there will be a lot of emotions.

After a few months, you will begin to miss your family, food, friends and the normal life you left behind. Without learning the new culture and confronted with a language barrier, a lot of people quit at this time because they cannot handle the emotional part. Within a few months they are back to their original habits and not willing to make any changes or efforts, they may have even gone back to their home country.

The weather could be another factor for you. In fact, it could be another essential part that gets you out of the game.

As you can see there are many factors one has to take into account when moving to a new country. With the knowledge I have from my own experiences and that of the many people I have helped immigrate to Canada, I have written this book. I hope it will serve as a helpful tool for you to make your trip or your move to another country, so that you can achieve your dreams.

I have provided you with a list of all of the key ideas from each chapter so that you can return to them whenever you wish.

CHAPTER 1

MAKING THE DECISION TO MOVE TO ANOTHER COUNTRY

I UNDERSTAND THAT ONE OF THE most difficult parts of immigrating is making the decision to move. This is not just you - it is difficult for everyone, but once you have done it then you can move to the next step. For example, when I think about going to the gym, running or hiking, it is very difficult for me to make this decision to go. But once I am there, I feel so blessed to have made the decision to go. This happens to me in most areas of my life. When things are not easy or I have to take a different road into the unknown, I get afraid and then drag things out until I get very sick and must move forward. During the last decade of my life, I have learned that I must decide to create action. Once I know what I want, then I can move forward to the goal. This will help me to move towards my future and to fulfill my purpose in this life.

Deciding it is not always easy, but I suggest you start by writing down the five reasons why you would benefit from moving to a new country. For example, you may list a better job, a better government system, a healthier environment, a richer country and so on. So when you have the five reasons, then write down five reasons why you don't want to live in the country or place you are living currently. For example, it could be such things as the weather, the neighbours, your job, or your culture, just to mention a few.

Then do a research of the place that you believe would help you to achieve some of the goals mentioned above and once you find it start making a 12-month plan for moving. How would you achieve your goals, and who do you know that could help you to achieve your goals? Do you have any friends or family members in the country you have chosen? Make sure you research communities, churches and other institutions that may be able to assist you in your settlement of this country or may assist you in finding better accommodations, schools for yourself or for your family and so on.

Remember the decision is the most difficult part, but just jump in and move forward. Allow yourself to live your own dream. Remember that this is your life, and you have the power and potential to live the life you want and to live your dream fully with all the potential you have available. You will never regret it. More importantly, life is very short and we are only here temporarily. Why not live a life of fulfilment and happiness?

WHEN IS THE RIGHT TIME TO TAKE ACTION?

The right time to act is today, right now, while you are reading these words. There will never be the perfect time and the perfect circumstances to make a move. You need to decide if this is for you. If your answer is yes, then continue reading this book because it has been designed for you. If your answer is no, this book is also designed for you, because at the end of this book, you may change your mind and want to take on this new adventure.

I have learned that life is too short to live worrying about anything and everything. More importantly, people stay in a miserable life that they hate and in a country where they don't like the system, the economy or social security because they are so afraid of making a change. They are frozen by the idea of moving out of their comfort zone, and that makes them incapable of making a decision.

These people always are waiting for the best time to make this decision, but unfortunately there is no such thing as a perfect time. There are a lot of challenges once you move to a new place, which causes a lot of people to quit before they have even really tried. When animals change from one habitat to another, it is very difficult for them. Some even become sick or die in this move. Of course, humans get scared and frustrated by not understanding the language, culture, food, and even the professional aspects of a new place.

You may not be doing or may never do the same thing that you did in your country of birth, but it is worth making the move if it will allow you to see your next generation happier. Even more important, you will see them growing up in a healthy country with a strong economy and with a strong respect for the culture of others. A country that provides people with a good quality of life is so important.

Since I never gave up, this will be my advice. Never, never, never give up because you will see the sun coming, even as the climb gets harder. In those moments when you think it is impossible, remember that you are getting ever closer to achieving your dream. Have a dream, but make sure you are originator and it is your dream, and not the dream of others. If it is your dream, no matter how many failures you have, then you will make it happen because you will refuse to let anything get in your way.

HANDLING FEAR

Fear is one of the emotions that paralyzes most of humanity. When people experience this emotion, they would rather leave their dreams on the side instead of dealing with the uncomfortable feelings of fear. The good news is that we all experience fear in life. However, a few of us do let fear become a barrier to our dreams. It is important that you acknowledge the fear and allow the emotion to be, but don't let it stop you from making your dream become a reality. I do remember that before coming to my adoptive country, I was full of doubt and fear about the unknown. The fear of failing, the fear of not being good enough for my parents and disappointing everyone, and the fear of knowing that I was stable and had a good job but I was leaving everything behind to make my dream happen. However, I allowed the feeling to be, but did not to allow it to destroy my dream. I was determined to come to my adoptive country and learn a second language, and to then go back and dedicate my life to research.

Fear is nothing but a way to identify that you are moving out of your comfort zone and moving towards your dream. If you are frozen by fear, the great news is this emotion is telling you that you are moving into the right direction towards your goal, your purpose, your mission and the rewards that are on the other side. Once you step into your fear and move forward, you are in the best position to receive the most amazing part of your rewards. You will be present in peace, love, and positivity. The universe will bend to your side to help you continue in the progressive realization of your mission.

OVERCOMING THE UNKNOWN

Overcoming the unknown is a very fun way to handle the fear because, while you are feeling fear, you are also accepting the challenge that comes with relocating to this unknown place. This is where you will find new friends, work, people, languages, culture, lifestyles and more.

The unknown is the most blessed part of the decision, because this is where the Universe takes care of our purpose and supports us to go through life without resistance. Here you will see the unknown take you in a different direction and be grateful for it, because you will discover a whole new way to live a fulfilling life.

After acknowledging the fear of the unknown and becoming comfortable with it, I advise you to take a map of the city, using it to explore and learn about your new home. Look at the map and watch videos about the city, activities and even the weather. This will help you to get to know the city, the businesses, and the grocery shops. Note the areas that are safe for shopping, or what to visit as tourist attractions and more. By studying that map and researching the city, you are challenging yourself to get to know more about the real culture and surroundings of your new home.

I remember when I first arrived in my new country. It was a beautiful summer day, so I woke up at 5:30 am and took a run around the beach for about 2 hours. I then sat on a bench and read a book in the sun. I noticed there were a lot of people running during the morning. There were no specific ages, but a variety of people from around the town that came to run that morning. Something that really got my attention was that people woke up this early for a walk with their dogs, which were like their children. For me this was weird, because in my birth country, dogs are not treated that well. Once I finished reading a few pages of my book, I looked at people watching and enjoying the beautiful weather, I then went back to my apartment and began cooking some food to leave for a long walk around the whole town. This was my routine for the first four weeks of my visit to that town, until everything looked so familiar that I was not afraid of the city. I knew the streets by memory. I knew where the train stations were, the food, the super market, the bakery, the coffee shop, the cheaper schools, and had learned almost all of the city by heart. I felt that I knew the city better than the residents and this helped me to overcome the unknown. I was feeling confident and safe, while I was getting used to the surrounding areas.

ARE YOU HEADING IN THE RIGHT DIRECTION?

You may wonder if you are heading in the right direction. It is important to check the list we made in the first section, in which we included our dreams and what could we change to make our lives better. Did following those dreams make you come over? Or are you feeling lost and homesick? Even getting into different habits and routines won't allow us to achieve our dreams, unless we use them to address the challenges we face. For me, my challenge was to learn the English language.

So three months after I landed, I reviewed my map and my plan. It was then that I discovered I was not learning as much English as I wanted to, because I was still living with my friend who spoke my mother tongue. This was not helping me to achieve my goal to learn the language of my new country. So I began putting up boundaries and changing my life accordingly. I asked my friend to not talk to me during the day. She could do her own stuff and I would do mine. That she must walk to different places than me, so that I was forced to use English.

After this date, instead of going home after school, I went to Tim Hortons (24 hours). I opened my computer, and I plugged into their Wi-Fi to watch movies in English with subtitles in English. I wrote down all the new words that I didn't know the meaning of, then I searched for the meaning, and then I copied pages of the same word and its meaning, until I had it memorized. After a few months, I began to understand the people around me and follow the full conversations. I could not communicate fully myself, even though I spoke a few words to survive. Certainly, I could understand the conversations almost fully after about six months of a few hours of sleep per day and avoiding any person who spoke my mother tongue.

When I said review your plan, it means making sure that you are redirecting your actions to achieve your plans for your new country and you should do these reviews roughly every three months. As part of my profession as an immigration consultant, I see a lot of people from different countries. No matter where they come from, they get lost if they don't review what motivated their decision or dream to come over or move to a different place. It is very easy to get lost and distracted with the beauty of the city and other changes, and then you ended up losing the purpose of your move. One year later, you go back to your home country full of frustration and regrets because you lost focus on your plan or forgot about it. This review is vital to achieving your dream and becoming successful in the new country, because it keeps you on task.

For example, I know some people that forget that they came with a plan and a purpose. Some of my clients reach 24 months in their new country and still haven't learned the language, because they forgot the purpose of learning the language. They have not completed any other goals. Some of them began working in an area that was not their profession and ended up staying in that job for years, even though this didn't fit into their original plan. As a result, they are frustrated and unhappy. Never accept anything less than what you have asked for. This is why you must review your plan and your dreams. I do it on a daily basis, but you need to start getting used to doing it every three months and make the necessary changes to adjust the original plan as needed.

12 MONTH BUDGETING PLAN

Budgeting yourself before coming to a new country is one of the most important things you should consider doing prior to moving. I would suggest learning about the currency and the exchange value prior to moving to the new country. You must have a budget and know how much you would need to spend for rent, food and other needs, such as school and travelling around visiting new places at least once a week. It is important that you travel around, so you can get to know the area and the culture.

I remember when I first came to my adoptive country, I spent a lot of money in rent, clothes, and eating. First, I was home-sick and I could justify my shopping by mentioning that I was missing my family, friends and place of birth. However, this is not true. I learned later that it is something called emotional intelligence, which means that my reward would come later once I have achieved my goal. Budgeting so you don't over spend your money is one of the smartest plans you can make prior coming to a new country. This would allow you not to acquire undesirable stuff that isn't necessary. In addition, you will have more money to help you towards your Permanent Resident goals. Especially if you are one of those individuals who is a professional, speaks English and wishes to become a Permanent Resident of the new country, then you must have a certain amount of money in the bank prior applying for your papers. Trust me, budgeting before coming to your country will make a big difference in your life and settlement.

MAKING FRIENDS

This is a very important point, but since you are in a new country and building a new life, you need to be smarter in choosing your friends. Please choose those people who can help you and encourage you to take your dream to the next level. We become who we associate with. If you came to this new place to become a millionaire, please make sure you surround yourself with entrepreneurs and business owners. If you came here to become more spiritual, surround yourself with churches, yoga places, spiritual temples and more. You become like the people you are surrounded by.

It is also important to mention that western countries have a diversity of cultures, so be open to new religions, ways of thinking, different languages, food and more. Coming from a poor country with a deeply religious culture, it was very difficult to accept other religions. Mexico is a very religious place, and I could not understand Muslims, Buddhists, Hindus and other types of religions. I thought the only religion that existed was Catholic. Of course, this is not true. As I began to be more open minded, I learned there are other types of religions. This is not good or bad, just different. I surrounded myself with new people. More importantly, I surround myself with positive people that would help me to achieve my dreams.

Since I love sports, I made friends with groups of hikers and bikers. I also attended churches of different religions, so I could get to know more about every culture and better understand my friends. It is also important to mention that through my profession as an Immigration Consultant (previously as a paralegal to a big law firm in Vancouver, BC, Canada), I have had to deal with people from different backgrounds, religions and countries. You can't deal with a Punjabi community the same way that you do a Latin community. Making different friends from different countries helped me to open my mind and respect others. Of course, it also makes me better able to serve them, because I could understand their culture and costumes, as well as what they liked and what they disliked. My clients are fascinated when I can tell them about their culture and religion. They like to know that I am knowledgeable and I am interested to know more about them and their previous country of origin.

Making friends is one of the most important parts in settling in another country. While you help others, others help you to achieve your dreams. You never know who can help you to access the next level! I have seen cases of immigrants that as soon as they settle have a multimillionaire business and they could help others through their business.

Make sure you choose properly. You can make the best decision because this is your choice to relocate and you get to choose your new home. The first time you didn't have the option to choose, because you were born in your birth country. But in your adoptive country, your life is your choice, including your friends and even your successes. They are your responsibility. Take control of your life and plan it, then make it happen. Your dreams will come true, I know this for a fact, if you persist, follow through your dreams, adjust on the way and continuously review your plan. Trust me, you are on the way to making your dreams happen and living your dreams to fully align with your purpose. Nothing better than to live a life that you have chosen and see your dreams becoming a reality.

BE PASSIONATE

It is passion that counts when you are moving to another place. I believe you must be passionate and do things from your heart. Why? Because if you are doing things that you are not passionate about, you are being forced to do it and your energy is not fully functioning at 100%. You want to be there 100%, when you are doing what you are passionate about. For example, if you are passionate about building houses for other people, and I use this as an example because many of my clients do construction, I always tell them how important their service is in our society. Without them, we wouldn't be able to have homes, schools, hotels, or bridges, so I tell them their services are valuable to us as a society. No matter what you do, you must be passionate about it. You must feel in your heart that you are doing it as a service, which you can do with or without pay. I heard from Rich Dad (Robert Kiyosaki) that the rich do not work for money. This makes so much sense, because when we do things from our heart, we could not be paid and still be happy and fulfilled. Trust me, once you find your passion, you will be able to achieve not only happiness but a lot of financial rewards. I know for a fact that money follows when you live in your passion. The Universe supports those who have a plan and are passionate about what they do.

I invite you to reflect on your passion before you move. Ask yourself the following questions:

1. Why I was sent into this body?
2. What was the purpose you were charged with?
3. If you don't know and you feel lost, ask for direction,

but remember to focus on what is your purpose for being here.

4. Are you passionate about what you do now? If not, why not? What are you willing to do to change this?

5. Are you living the life of your dreams?

6. Where is the place you would love to live? What do your finances looks like? How much money do you wish to have once you live there? When will be the right time to reach for your financial goals? What is the service you will provide in exchange of this money?

7. How many people and/or lives are you willing to impact?

For now, to answer these questions, close your eyes and be open and willing to receive the answer that comes, so you can have the life you are looking for. I know a lot of you will tell me that you feel nothing and you could not do the exercise. After talking with thousands of clients from different countries, I see one similarity in all of them – it does not matter which country, culture and so on. They all let their minds take over, and the mind does not always serve in the process of achieving your dream of moving to a different country to have the life you always have dreamed about. Quiet your brain, breathe deeply and try again - this is an important part of your success, believe me.

I want to share a small part of my life. My original plan was to learn English and then go back to my birth country and continue to work for my doctorate degree in law. Unfortunately, I was not that lucky and English became a challenge. It was very difficult to learn and speak English. I will say that I am still learning. If you are one of my clients and hear me speaking, you know that after a decade, I still make mistakes. Since I am not a quitter, I didn't want to go back until I could master the language and I still have not mastered it. Canada has become my second home. Was this easy? No, it was not easy - it was very difficult in all aspects in my life. But I remember that I wrote a plan on a piece of paper. This is the first time I set out to learn how to plan.

I listed all the things I would love to have, I set dates to achieve those things, and guess what? Two years later, everything that I set down on the list has become a reality. I met the love of my life and my soul mate, the one who the universe actually did choose to help me to achieve all my dreams. I was in the job that I wanted with the right mentors and support, living in the country that I wanted, and all this without even speaking English well. Do you see all the excuses that you may have created to not have what you deserve?

So quiet your mind and begin dreaming and putting into action what you need to turn those dreams into reality. In the next few chapters, I will talk more about other experiences that led me to making my dreams come true. Continue reading so you can achieve success and all the things you want. Next, I will tell you how I ended up living in the house of my dreams and making a lot of money.

CHAPTER 2

SETTLING IN A NEW COUNTRY

SOCIAL MEDIA

TODAY, IN THIS NEW ERA of information, you must be an active user of the new ways of communicating and marketing yourself, so the community gets to know about you and you get to know about them as well, and what better place to do this than social media (i.e. Facebook, LinkedIn, Instagram).

However, in life there are limitations and we must set the rules. You should only view these sites for 20 to 30 minutes per day and it is preferable to do it at the same time of day every day. The reason is to avoid them becoming a big distraction in your life, because that won't help you to achieve your goals.

Also, newspapers are great for finding out if there is another win for your soccer team, but it is also good to get away from all the bad news found in newspapers that won't help you to stay motivated. I usually read about finances, schooling, and cultural events and then I close the newspaper. In all countries, I have learned there is good news and bad news.

KNOWING THE GOVERNMENT INSTITUTIONS THAT CAN PROVIDE HELP

It is important to be familiar with the government institutions where you can find help. Just to mention a few:

1. Health Care institutions and rules
2. Police Departments
3. Institutions offering settlement services for immigrants
4. Banks and what they offer.
5. Immigration Rules, if it is your intention to live in this place as a Permanent Resident. It is important to visit a lawyer or consultant that can provide you with a clear assessment of your case.
6. Churches and communities

In every country, there are government institutions that can help you to settle and make the process easier.

HOW TO IMMERSE IN THE LANGUAGE AND CULTURE

This is a very important topic, because if you are living in a foreign country, you need to learn the language of that country. There are different ways to do so, but it is critical that you have a clear picture of when and how you will make the immersion and that it happen as quickly as possible.

It is important that for the first months, you start taking some classes in a formal class room. This is why it is important to have your budget in place - to be able to concentrate on immersing yourself in school.

There are other changes that you must consider if you are really taking this seriously. One of them is that you must get away from your mother tongue. What I mean is that you must not speak with any person that speaks the same language you do. This won't help you to achieve your goal. **Rule number one is to speak only with people that do not speak your language**, but speak the language you are trying to learn - this will help to force your mind to practice the language.

Another tip - it is important that you watch television or radio only in the language that you are immersing in, even if you don't understand it. Trust me, this will help a lot in learning the new language. I recommend that you watch one movie daily with subtitles for the language you are learning, then write down in a note book all the words that you do not understand. Once the movie is over, search in Google Translator for the meaning of that word in the language you are learning. Once you have the meaning of the word, write that word 200 times, move forward with the next one and complete the process again.

It is vital that you move forward with the language and advance as much as you can. I have been working with immigrants for the past 11 years. It does not matter which language they speak or which culture they have come from, when they apply this method, one year later they are generally fluent in speaking their new language. There are exceptions, of course, of people who can learn to speak the language even faster, but usually it takes about a year. However, there are others that do not apply the process, but continue living with people that speak the same language and practice the same habits as they do. I meet these people years later, and they still have not changed jobs or grown financially because they never wanted to experience the pain of moving away from their **comfort zone**. They are unhappy and frustrated, because after several years, they are living in another country with thousands of opportunities that they cannot enjoy because they choose not to pay the price that comes with learning a new language.

As I explained in my previous chapters, there is a price for everything we do in life. We need to become aware of these prices and balance them into what we are envisioning in our future. For example, if you want to live a different life, understand the culture of the place you are moving to, and live as a citizen of that country, you need to try to leave behind your friends and your comfort zone. I understand your frustration - there are times when you cannot speak with anyone, because nobody understands what you said. You start feeling lonely and homesick, then the doubter part that exists in you starts to question if you made the right decision in moving to this country. It is important that you remain aware during the process, and that you remember that this is just temporary - that you will be able to communicate in the next few months, if you just keep applying the process.

Last but not least, once you move to another country, you need to close that chapter in your life and only contact a few people back in your home country. For example, your parents and siblings would be on that list. I have known clients that move and contact their friends almost every day like they are still living in their home countries, because those friends were not aware that they were moving. Because of this, they didn't close those chapters in their lives. Another important example is leaving a relationship behind that brings a lot of confusion and distraction for the person that is moving to the unknown country. You either move with your partner or you terminate that relationship completely before you move, otherwise you will be stuck for a long time, unable to move forward in your new life.

This is important for you to consider no matter if you are still planning to move, or if you have already moved to a new country. It is relevant if you want to succeed. If you are making or have made one of the mistakes I spoke about above, this is your opportunity to become aware and make the move to change and start again. It is never too late.

It is sad to see people go back to their regular lives in the country of their birth, unhappy and frustrated with the government system because they are not willing to step outside of their comfort zone and go through the painful process of change. Trust me, it is a journey of growth; mental, spiritual, physical and emotional. You will not only end up stronger and more aware of how you live and your dreams, but you will also become financially rich. It is worth the move. There is pain, but it is worth the rewards ahead.

BANKING

It is important to be able to transfer and move your money from your birth country to your new country. However, you must do some research before you making the move. One of the reasons is that there are several institutions, and you need to consider the fees they are charging and what is convenient for you. In addition, there are exchange rates that you need to consider. Before you open a new bank account, you should ask all these questions of your bank:

1. What is the monthly fee you will be charging?

2. What are the different benefits that you are offering that other banks do not offer?

3. What is the exchange rate for other currencies?

4. What are the loans that your bank offers for businesses or to purchase a property?

5. How can I know you will keep your word in providing me what you promised today into the future?

6. If I am unhappy with your services and account, can I close my account without any extra charges or fines?

It is important that you ask several questions before you open the bank account to avoid extra charges. Remember that every penny counts when you move to a new country, so you must make sure you inquire about all these details before signing onto any bank, especially if you have money in your country that you want to transfer.

MORTGAGE

As soon as you can get yourself a mortgage, please make that move. Look at the initial value of the property as an investment, as you make money overtime when you buy property. Of course, make sure to investigate to find a property that you like and can get the best deal on.

First, describe and make a list describing the place you would love to have. For example:

1. Where do I want to be located, in the forests or by a river? Do you want something with a view or this does not matter to me? Do you want to be in a rural or suburban area or in the city? Does your new home need to be a house or can it be an apartment?

2. How many rooms do I want and need at this moment and over the next five years?

3. How much can I afford to pay monthly?

4. What is the price range I am comfortable with and can afford according to my income? It is important that you consider all the expenses behind buying a property, such as insurance, government fees, lawyer fees, and banks fees. However, do not allow your **fear to be in the middle of this move.** As soon as you feel ready, start looking for a property and a bank or broker that will lend you the money for the purchase.

5. **Does this place have rooms to rent, or if it is a house, a basement to rent? If it is an apartment or townhouse, make sure you question if it is legal to have tenants in the building. There are a lot of regulations on these places, so you must first consider all these questions before making the move to purchase a place.**

Purchasing a property as soon as you can will save you thousands of dollars in paying rent and you will see the increasing value of your investment in the future, especially in places where real state is always going up. You are making an investment, using your money to pay the mortgage instead of paying rent. As soon as you can, make that move and don't let fear in the middle of this situation. Acknowledge the fear and remember that we all feel it. This is a game of managing your emotions and making the move even though you feel frozen. There is a small difference between unsuccessful and successful people. The successful don't let their fear stop them from making a decision and making moves. The unsuccessful don't like the unknown and allow that fear to stop them, thinking that where they are is safe.

LOCAL EVENTS, COMMUNITIES AND CHURCHES PLAY A BIG ROLE

It is important that you are informed about what is happening in your community through churches, events, and other avenues. The reason why this is important is because the more you are aware of the needs for the community, the more you can benefit by providing them with your services. What do I mean by this? Well, communities have needs. They need an accountant for people who have businesses, but they also require bookkeepers, lawyers, architects, constructions workers, and cleaners, just to mention a few. So you can start thinking about a bigger vision – how you can use your profession to serve others. Remember that the more people you can serve, the more financial freedom you can have. For example, if you are a bookkeeper, then you could start charging a reasonable fee to business owners on a monthly basis and they will benefit, but the key for success is how many people you can serve. For example, banks have low monthly fees. They could range from 5 dollars per month to 35 dollars per month, but the reason why banks are wealthy is because they serve millions of people. That is where you need to become creative and think, "What can I do to serve as many people as I can with an affordable fee, so that we all benefit from my services?"

Be creative and remember that as an immigrant, you have advantages. Most immigrants are bilingual or trilingual, so you can use this to your advantage and serve the communities that speak the same languages that you speak. I explained in previous chapters that you must get away from your community and people that speak your mother tongue to learn a new language, but now you can actually serve them.

It is relevant that you also consider yourself as an advantage because, as I explained before, you are one of the survivors that make their dreams it happen, by deciding to move, settling in a new country, and learning a new language.

You are strong emotionally, mentally, financially and physically. Trust me, I have seen many immigrants come into this country and I can see the difference between those who succeed and those who fail. The differences are small but determinant.

So always see yourself as the winner of the war, if you are still in the country you planned to move to or if you haven't moved but are thinking of moving, then you have the advantage of benefiting yourself through this book. **Read the tips, the examples, and most importantly, take action.**

One day, I heard that success is a learnable skill. Today, I can tell you with confidence that it is a learnable skill. Everyone on this planet can become successful, if we become aware of our fears, thoughts and the actions that we take in this life.

It is vital that you continue reading the next chapter, which includes new tips, stories and examples. It is valuable for you to read this, and apply the tools that certainly can help you to achieve your goals quicker and easier. It is like a GPS - you have the map to navigate through, without being alone.

CHAPTER 3

OVERCOMING THE CHALLENGE OF UPGRADING YOUR EDUCATION

THERE ARE MANY PEOPLE WHO come from different countries with college degrees, Masters' degrees and PhD's. However, when they arrive, they don't know that they can upgrade their education in their adopted country. There are institutions where your previous education can be evaluated, and you will learn exactly what your studies from your birth country are equal to in your new country.

There are certain requirements that must be followed to complete the assessment. One of them is to submit a copy of all your documents. For example: transcripts, certificate, diploma, or degree with all the translations from the original language to English or the language that is spoken in your new country. Almost all the places will require you to create an online account and make a payment. The system will automatically give you a copy of the payment with a number. You must request all your transcripts and degrees from the University you studied at, and request them to be sent in a sealed envelope, directly to the institution that is evaluating your documents.

There are several differences to be aware of when you need to evaluate and transfer your degree as an engineer, accountant, architect, or lawyer, just to mention a few. Is it much faster to obtain the equivalency of these degrees from your country to this country? Of course, there is also a difference depending on your home country. For example, if you have a degree from a Latin American country, rather than if you are immigrating from Australia, Western Europe or even the USA, the transfer can involve more work. The transfer of a degree from another English-speaking country could be just to take a test and/ or study a few courses, even online, to get your license here. However, Latin American countries, especially Central and South American ones, have many differences when transferring your education from one place to another. Some degrees will only require you to study for a one-year master degree and then take a couple courses online, and you can be ready to take a test from the regulator.

However, there are other professions that are way more complicated, such as doctors, pharmacists, dentists and more. These take a lot of study, money and years to get completed and allow you to practice in the western world.

I find there is a contradiction on this, because on the one side there is a high demand for these careers. The government even provides avenues for doctors to enter to Canada. On the other hand, once they are in this country, they are not allowed to practice and the process to become a doctor is long and expensive.

As I mentioned earlier, with the years of experience that I have serving people to immigrate to Canada, I have met a lot of professionals in this area who have been trying for years to get their license to practice here. However, as I mentioned above, if you have made your intentions clear, no matter how difficult it seems, never give up and you will be able to achieve your dreams.

Here are the names of the institutions that can help you to evaluate your schooling.

You can get your assessment from:

Comparative Education Service – University of Toronto School of Continuing Studies (Date designated: April 17, 2013)

International Credential Assessment Service of Canada (Date designated: April 17, 2013)

World Education Services (Date designated: April 17, 2013)

International Qualifications Assessment Service (Date designated: August 6, 2015)

International Credential Evaluation Service (Date designated: August 6, 2015)

Medical Council of Canada (professional body for Doctors) (Date designated: April 17, 2013)

Pharmacy Examining Board of Canada (professional body for Pharmacists) (Date designated: January 6, 2014)

The institutions above are just to mention a few.

There are a lot of people that get lost and they don't know if they can continue.

If you feel that you will get lost once you are in the new country, stop, breathe and find somewhere you can be quiet and feel peaceful. When we are stressed, tired, mad, frustrated, and overwhelmed, we don't make the best decisions. We feel we cannot move forward. This is why I love the book, *The 7 Habits of Highly Effective People*. The last habit mentioned in the book is hugely important:

SHARPEN THE SAW

"Balance and renew your resources, energy, and health to create a sustainable, long-term, effective lifestyle. It primarily emphasizes exercise for physical renewal, good prayer (meditation, yoga, etc.) and good reading for mental renewal. It also mentions service to society for spiritual renewal." – *The 7 Habits of Highly Effective People*

When you are feeling overwhelmed, remember to stop and sharpen your soul and your body and renew everything before you continue. My work requires a lot of mental effort, so over the years I have learned to stop and sharpen myself and give time for my body to renew and to clear. Once I am back, I feel more vigorous, more present, more aware, and sensitive. I am able to serve others better, because I have served myself first. I am writing this because I truly believe and practice this habit on a regular basis. I used to practice it only twice every year. Now, I can sense the benefits, so I practice it once every two to three months according to my schedule. My goal in the next few years is to be able to do it on a monthly basis, spend one week by myself sitting on the beach, sharpening my soul and my body. Certainly, practicing this principle gives me creativity and brings out the best of me.

I love the following example: A person who was a philosopher spent most of his time looking like he was not doing anything. He gazed out of the window for hours, sat doing nothing, and made no attempt to look busy. This drove the other philosophers up the wall and they complained to their boss. The boss became interested at this report, and asked them how long this behavior had been going on. He told the other philosophers to see if they could provide this philosopher with coffee or lunch, anything to make sure his day wouldn't be interrupted. The other philosophers became irate over this preferential treatment. The boss told them that the last time he acted like this, and the time before, and the time before this, he came up with great ideas that were worth millions of dollars and served to improve the technology of the world.

You see some times when you quiet your mind or sharpen your soul, you come up with the best ideas. I practice this when I have a case that I need to present into the immigration tribunals. I read the laws and case laws, sit with my client and ask several questions, then I sit and quiet my mind. My higher self gives me the answer of how to solve the process and/or the questions I should ask in the tribunals and how I should approach the case. I have learned to be still and find the answer. However, before I used to try to solve it by myself by reading and overwhelming myself. This would lead to me becoming over tired, bringing negative results and frustration. Once I learned to rely on my infinitive intelligence that comes from my connection with the universe, I learned to relax and breathe. Once these emotions pass, I move on.

FOLLOW UP WITH A PROGRAM THAT IS SIMILAR IN A LOCAL UNIVERSITY

I have discovered that the current educational system was created for the Industrial Era. Why do I say this? Because I believe education was created to train you to become an employee. I recall all my schooling, from grade 4 to grade 12, and all I remember I heard from my teachers was, "What would you like to study? You need to choose your education carefully, and choose the degree you wish to study with intention, because you may not be able to find work later if you don't!" Or they used to say, "If you are a singer, painter, or artist, you may not be able to find work later!" So the educational system was created for the Industrial Era. However, we are entering into a different Era - some people call it the Era of Information, others called the Era of Illumination. Whichever it is, it is clear to me that the educational system needs to make some adjustments to be able to bring out the best of each person. After so many years in school, we should complete college or university with satisfaction, knowing our higher potential, either as entrepreneurs or employees, but acting on what our real skills are.

After so many years advising people from all over the world, I find a lot of unhappy people, who are frustrated because they chose the wrong career and they are working in a job they don't like. We choose jobs we don't like over following our passions, because school trains us to be afraid, especially if we want to be a singers or artists, because we are told there are few jobs like that. Also, schools teach us to work individually and compete against each other, instead of inspiring us to work as a team and become great leaders. We aren't taught to look deep inside ourselves and be motivated to do what we would like, and forget about whether there is a job or not in the area. I truly believe that when you are in your higher selves, if something does not exist, then you can create it. So if there is not work in the area that you desire to work in, you can create it because you are living your truth and you are loyal to your higher potential.

For decades school has been more damaging than serving to humanity. Perhaps you feel you studied something you didn't choose, or it was chosen by the influence of your parents or teachers or friends, and you feel you hate to do what you do. You feel tired all the time, or more importantly sick. I invite you to stop and search deep inside yourself to find what area you really would like to spend the rest of your days in. Even if you don't get paid, you will get up from bed being grateful and happy to do it. Some of you will know the answer right away, and will find clarity very soon. Others of you will be confused and won't know the answer.

Don't worry, keep meditating and questioning yourself, even making a list of all the things that you do naturally, all the abilities and the skills that you have, and then ask yourself, "Which of these things I would apply on my profession or like to do on a regular basis?" If you find yourself sick, depressed, lonely, hopeless and so on, then of course, you are not living up to your potential. Stop as soon as you can and find what it is that you would love to do. I guarantee you that as soon as you take action and stop worrying about your fears, such as how you would eat, pay your bills and so on, the universe will bend and work as fast as possible to bring you all the necessary things that you need to live and, more importantly, to step into your higher self.

I would rather know I had wasted 5 years in university, than spend the rest of my life doing something that I hate doing. This is the case of many recent graduates, because I do have a lot of clients that come to this country once they graduate. However, if you are a person that is over 50 and it happen to be reading this book, it is not an accident if this book is talking to you. It is never too late to make a change in your life, step into your higher potential and find the power within you.

Now, if you are one of the lucky ones that studied what you love and you would love to serve your community, then this is also for you. I will advise you to study something related to what you love in your new country. Study it in a short course, with a certificate or diploma, to be able to step into your career quickly. The reason I am telling you this is because if they hire you into a company, they will always mention that you need to have some education in your new country to justify the promotion. So it is recommended that as soon as you can, you choose the school and the course and then begin. With the new era of technology, at least in the Western countries, there are a lot of online courses that will be valid. They are so well designed for you to learn in the comfort of your own home, thus saving you a lot of time in commuting from one place to another.

It is important that you research if the school that you choose has a program with a good reputation in the area you will be studying. What I mean by this is, there are schools that are known for degrees in Physiology, and there are others that are known for engineering degrees, even though they offer Administration degrees too.

VOLUNTEER IN A FIELD SIMILAR TO YOUR PROFESSION

There are people that always ask me if they should volunteer in the area of their profession. If you are under a temporary status, you need to research before you volunteer. In some Western countries, volunteering could be considered work, even if you are not getting paid for the position. What do I mean by this? If you work, even if it is not paid, you can be breaking the laws and working illegally. For example, a church is a good way to provide volunteer work. On the other hand, if you are volunteering with an accounting company, performing bookkeeping tasks without having the right work permit, and you are there for 8 hours, then this is considered work, even if you don't get paid.

This is why volunteer work should be carefully reviewed, especially if you are on temporary status. However, if you are a Permanent Resident or a citizen of the country, then of course volunteering is a great way to gain experience and step into your profession in a foreign country. I guarantee you that after 3 to 6 months, if you take this seriously, you will be able to get a job in that company. But you must be able to walk the extra mile, to show the value that your work has, to be present and give 100 percent of your capabilities. My best managers are those who were present in my office and told me that they want to practice without pay and show me that they can work the extra mile. If there is no work, then they make it happen and create it. They are the ones who become my managers or partners in my business; those who are willing to do the work no matter what the cost is.

WHEN TO MAKE A MOVE AND SHOULD YOU ACCEPT LESS IN WAGES COMPARED TO OTHERS?

In the first years of working, you may not get as high of a wage as you wish. However, the experiences you gain will be much more valuable than completing a whole Master's degree. Work experience in the Western world is very important to employers. This is why getting paid lower wages for the first 2 to 3 years is totally acceptable.

However, if after that time, you are still getting the same salary, then you need to step up and ask for feedback from the company. You can ask them what the opportunities are available for you to serve in other departments, or if you could have more responsibility within the company.

Ask them what you can do to make more money? How do you find my work and performance so far? Do you think after 3 years of working for your company and giving what I believe is my 100 percent, I am valuable to you? How can I serve more? You will get the feedback; especially if you have a manager who is honest. They may tell you if your performance has been average, and that is why your salary is on that level. He may tell you that he will think of other potential opportunities for you to work inside the company, or ask you what the position you wish to have.

They may ask you how much money you want to make, so you need to be ready to have the answer for them to provide you what you need. For example, if they ask you what you are looking for in a position or salary, you must be able to answer with clarity – "I would like to be the director of the company, or the president or the manager, and I would like to make $200,000 per year." Your answer must be clear.

CHAPTER 4

IMMERSING YOURSELF IN A NEW LANGUAGE AND CULTURE

PERSONAL EXPERIENCES

I WANT TO SHARE WITH YOU my personal experiences with learning a new language. The following method I will share I believe is the best way to learn a second language - through repetition and practice. When I came to Canada for the first time, I didn't speak any English at all. However, the deal was to come to Canada to learn the language because I was expecting to learn it to continue my PhD in Mexico. Nevertheless, learning a second language with my dyslexia was more complicated than what I thought. It was very difficult for me, until I actually applied the repetition and sub-conscious method that I am about to share with you. When using the school method, I was spending thousands of dollars and not getting ahead. I thought to myself, "How did I learn Spanish?" I learned very naturally and by repeating the words, and saying them several times until I could communicate.

The steps I recommend are as follows:

1. First, get away from all the people that speak your first language; this will push or force you to move forward with learning the language of your new country. This may make you feel homesick and, from time to time, you will want to quit and go back to your country, because you are missing your parents, friends, culture and language. I want to let you know that all this is only temporary and those emotions and feelings will disappear after time.

2. Second, pick a movie that you enjoy watching and watch it over and over from the beginning to the end. Put your earphones on and then set the subtitles in the language you want to learn. In my case this was English, but in your case this could be any other language you are learning. I guarantee you that you will get ahead in your learning skills if you implement my teachings. Write down all the words from the movie that you don't know the meaning of, or you are unable to understand. Write the words in a notebook. Once the movie is over, search for the meaning of your list of words and then write them in your notebook. Then, write that word and meaning over and over again for five pages once you have defined it. Trust me, this method helped me so much that in a few months I was able to understand most of the conversations on the street even though I could not speak at that time. I was able to understand what people wanted. I continued to repeat the same process over and over again; picking a new movie every month, watching the movie, writing down all the words that I was unaware and then finding the meanings and transcribing them. I repeated these steps because it seems simple, however, a lot of people quit before they even try, because it is

difficult. I can tell you that it is easy if you follow my steps, and are disciplined on the steps. You will master the second language and soon enough, you will be able to integrate into your new society.

3. Third, once you start understanding other people's conversations, then you will be able to start speaking the words. Then your brain automatically stores the new information you provide and you can pronounce new words. Don't worry too much about the accent you have at this point, because this won't help you. The more concerned you are about your pronunciation, the less you will want to practice, and then suddenly you find yourself depressed because you are unable to communicate. It is even sadder settling in a new country unable to speak the language and communicate. This will not only stop you from achieving success, but also will limit your opportunities to immerse yourself in a new culture.

Without understanding the language, you will limit yourself in work and business opportunities, just to mention a few. Getting ahead with the language will help you to increase your chances of success. It is worth the ride, I am telling you. I came to Canada with zero English speaking skills, with no previous education in the second language, and I can write it, speak it, and communicate effectively today. This last sentence is the most important, because in every language, if you don't know how to communicate effectively then you are not getting your point across.

4. Fourth, once you are communicating, keep repeating the same steps over and over again, but implement one more step: READ anything you can have access to- newspapers, books, and blogs. This will increase your brain's capacity to implement new words or remember the ones you have studied previously

and keep them in your brain. This will help your vocabulary to continue to increasing.

THE MOST CHALLENGING WORK

The most challenging work is not the physical - it is an emotional challenge that people have. Overcoming FEAR is the most challenging work that people have to learn to handle first. People get stuck in their fear and do not move forward because of the unknown.

What is the definition of fear?

An unpleasant, often strong, emotion caused by anticipation or awareness of danger.

According to the definition, fear is a dangerous feeling, the unknown, thinking that it is difficult, and thinking that is dangerous.

It is important to be aware of your emotions, whether it is positive or negative emotions, but then handle those emotions and the fear that you can have by making the decision to make your dreams a reality. There are many people, I will say more than 99.99 percent that get frozen by fear and get stuck in their comfort zone. They never act and move toward their dreams. They died with the wish in their hearts, "What if I was brave enough to do it? What if I had taken the chance of stepping into the unknown and moving towards my dream? What will it be with my life?" A lot of people live other people's dreams but not their own dreams, because the fear is in the middle. They are so afraid to make any decisions in their lives.

I encourage you to stop and think when you are experiencing this emotion. Just become aware of the feeling, and then stop thinking. Quiet your mind and just meditate on the reasons for you to go and visit or travel or immigrate to another country. What are the reasons? Are those YOUR reasons and dreams? Do you want to learn about a new culture? Language? And new lifestyle? Would you like to have a better governmental system?

If the answer of those questions is yes, then take the risk and the chance of moving or just traveling to another place. You won't regret it, because your mind and experiences will expand and increase in an amazing way that you cannot imagine. You will become more creative because you have experienced other cultures, other places, diversity and another language. You can now see life differently, and more importantly, you will be able to handle your fear at a different level. Next time, when you experience this emotion, you will handle it in a different way. The emotions will remain there forever, whether they are positive or negative, they will remain there. However, the fear will be less each time and less painful. What do I mean by this? Fear works as a muscle, and the more you exercise, the less painful it is. When you go to the gym for the first time, or running, or training, you have pain for the next week, especially if you stop going or moving forward but if you keep exercising regularly the pain disappears. Fear works the same way - the more chances and risks you take, the less painful it is, and guess what? Life becomes more fun and easy!

It is impressive and incredible how much you will learn by handling the emotion of fear, and how much further you will move towards success in your life. Success in your life is different from other people's success. For some of you, success is having a family and being able to be close to your children and wife or husband. For others, it is making a difference in this world, and for others, success is their profession. You may see success as becoming a millionaire or billionaire, or you may see it as being able to provide encouragement to others, or to learn from books. Whatever your dream is, make it happen. You only have one life and you only get one chance. Don't let fear freeze you and stop you from being what you want or who you want to become. Step into your mission in life and make it happen no matter what! What is it that you dream? Take a minute to answer this question.

Many of you may be unsure or wondering what your mission or purpose in this life is. I know, I have been there too. It is hard to know what you want, but it is easy to find out by failing and trying different things until you find the mission or purpose in your life.

Listen to your heart and to your emotions when you are doing what you love to do. For example, if you are an accountant and dislike numbers or helping companies to save money or figuring out problems with taxes, then you are definitely not fulfilling your mission. You may be only doing this work because your parents are accountants, or because you do not have another option or because you were not accepted into medical school. I don't know the reason but I know that are thousands of people that are not doing what their mission in life is, they are just living what life brings. If you feel like that, and with this book and want to make a pivot in your life, trust me it is never too late to make a change and step into your dream life.

TAKE ADVANTAGE OF THE MULTICULTURALISM

When you move to a place that is multicultural, where there are people with different backgrounds, each of them provides a particular advantage. Also, from a business perspective, take advantage of living in a multicultural place as a way to create more business. For example, if you are from China and live in Vancouver, BC, Canada, you will find out that it is an advantage for those who speak Mandarin or Cantonese. When they provide services to the Chinese community, they end up serving a big market because the community is so big.

The same example applies for people from Latin countries, the Middle East, and so on - when you can speak a second language and can provide services to this community, you are also able to provide those services to other communities. This is vital for growing your business and also to promote your business in your community.

Other advantages of living in a multicultural place are that you can learn about other perspectives or ways to see life. Through my own experiences, I have noticed something interesting - that every culture has their own beliefs, and that all of them teach a path to create good.

Furthermore, living around people from different countries creates a lot of fun in a new place to live, because there is a diversity of food, languages, cultures, and colours. This helps you to expand your mind and beliefs. I love the idea of communication with people that have come from other countries. While in my office, I help a lot of people to immigrate to Canada and, based on their backgrounds, I often provide them with different advice. For example, if someone comes from a Middle Eastern country where you can actually marry by arrangement from the parents, it is believable for the government to accept this marriage versus a client who is coming from a country where arranged marriages are uncommon. So I cannot advise my clients to apply and have an arranged marriage, for example, if they are from a Latin country.

Always keep your mind open to possibilities and how you could help others, no matter what their culture, beliefs, race or languages are. While you are doing this, you are helping yourself to move further as a person, and also as an owner of a company. I remember when I first came to my adoptive country, there were so many things I could not understand about others' cultures. There were also many things that happened which I perceived as weird. In reality, the things that happened were not out of the ordinary, but they were things I had never seen before in my home country. Multiculturalism can impact your life and expand your perceptions about other cultures and countries, and help you to see that there are many other places to live and that they may think differently than you.

RECOGNIZE THE ADVANTAGES

Recognize the advantage that you have if you are already in a new country with a different culture. Instead of seeing yourself as a person who does not speak the language (English or any other), see yourself as having the advantage of speaking a second language or learning a second language. This is a great advantage for professionals and business owners. Even though you do not speak the language perfectly, or if you have an accent, you still have an advantage over a lot of other people.

No matter what happens, always see yourself as having an advantage over local people. Why do I say this? It is very sad to see immigrants that do not speak the local language, that haven't involved themselves in their community or immersed themselves in the new place. They are still living like they had never left their home countries, regardless of the cost and price this brings to them. They do not want to move out of their comfort zone and they do not want to make any extra effort to get out of their minds and just learn the new language and immerse themselves in this new multicultural place.

I put a lot of emphasis on learning the new language of your new country because this is the most challenging part for people and a very important factor to your success. Without the ability to speak the language, they are unable to integrate into the new society and later on, they will feel excluded and live an unhappy life in the new culture. There is a saying in my home town that goes, "Wherever you travel, act like the people in that community." It takes effort, determination and a lot of discipline to make it happen, but I guarantee if you learn the language, then you are steps ahead of the game. Remember this phrase: if I can do it, you can do it. I learned from my mentors and I implemented their lessons in my daily life.

While I am meditating, I remember to be aware and present at all times. Due to my personality, I like to multitask, but I have been learning that keeping myself busy does not mean I am having a productive day or I am accomplishing more things. I have implemented into my life the idea to just be and remain present at all times. This is a great advantage that you can implement into your life anywhere you are. Focus and have the intention to accomplish one thing while you sit and do it. I have a very busy life; however, I am supported by and indebted to the wonderful team at my office that are always there to serve and help. More importantly, they are living their passions and dreams and that is a win for them.

When you take advantage of seeing all that surrounds you as positive and that all the events are happening around you for a reason, then you attract those people to your life who can help you to achieve your dreams. Together is the magic word - nobody alone has achieved massive success. It is only with a great team that you can do amazing things. It is an amazing place where you can do many things that can help others. When you have the intention to serve, the world bends to you and serves you - it works the other way around. We love to be served rather than serve, but when you wish and do it from your heart, the world will bend to you and serve you.

Take advantage of any situation that you are living in. I am not sure what is your fear or your struggle, but whatever your challenges are, there can be greater wins if you actually view them this way and change how you view these things.

It is all about perception - if you perceive a happy, successful, abundant, healthy and wealthy life, then that is what you end up having. Unfortunately, if you see the opposite, then that is what you will attract. That is why I suggest taking advantage of anything that comes into your life. Trust me, it works.

DON'T BE AFRAID TO MAKE MISTAKES

Unfortunately, we have been brought up with the idea of punishment or embarrassment if we make a mistake in this life. At the school where I grew up, the education system scored me and, if I made a mistake, they reminded me to get better for my next assignment, because otherwise I will fail the class. I remember I had to study hard and follow the rules in the school system, even though I did not agree with what I saw.

In our society and family, we are pushed to not make any mistakes or to fail in a business or project, because then you will be seen as a loser. However, I have had the blessing to learn from people who are wealthy, successful and creators of the biggest inventions. By reading their histories, I have learned that they failed many times before they actually had the invention and success they wished for. You may wonder if I have failed in life? The answer is yes, I have failed many times. I have tried several new things before getting to where I am today.

For example, I finished my degree in law and I had a very comfortable life in Mexico. I worked for the Government of my state, and held a good position with a salary. I owned a new car at that time, but I chose not to live that life. Instead I chose a life that was full of uncertainty about where I was heading. I had never been in Canada before and, more importantly, I did not speak any English at all. Regardless of all this, I made the decision to come to my new country. At first, it was only to learn the language, but thereafter, it became my home. Did I struggle and fail? Of course, I did. In fact, I didn't learn English in 6 months, as I had planned, but I saw this only as a temporary defeat. Do I speak perfect English? Of course not, but I don't think anyone does in this multicultural country - it is more important to speak a second language than to only speak native English. Even my neighbours or locals tell me how much they wish they could speak Spanish.

Making mistakes is totally fine in this life. Only by failing you can discover your purpose, what you really want for this life and what your mission is to accomplish. Missions are very important in your life because by living your mission, you can actually connect with your highly spiritual part and have everything you wish for. Keep reading into the next chapter, because you will unlock the power that comes from finding your mission and have everything you wish in material and spiritual ways.

CHAPTER 5

FINDING YOUR NICHE

THIS IS SOMETHING THAT YOU must keep in mind when you are in your new country. How can you do something that you like to do? In previous chapters, I talked about the mission or purpose that you have in life. It is important to mention that finding the profession that complements what you wish to do is extremely relevant to that mission or purpose.

Something that I noticed regarding the upgrade of your education is that for some people it is easier, for others it is not and for some professionals, it is almost impossible. For example, an engineer can upgrade his education, and so can an architect and an accountant. However, doctors are much more complex and require several years to complete the requirements to upgrade their education. For doctors, it is not only expensive, but there is also a lot of time to be invested and other requirements. The following is what I see a lot of immigrants do when their education takes a long time and they need to invest a lot of money, but of course, they love their professions and want to remain in that field.

Successful immigrants become creative; doctors take a short course as a nurse and, in this way, are able to enter into the medical industry sooner than they would by getting their doctor upgrade. These people end up getting good benefits, good wages and, more importantly, they are doing what they love to do. Furthermore, they start fulfilling all the requirements to upgrade their education. They are inside the industry, so it is easier for them to get their upgrade. This is a great tip to upgrade your education in a smart way, especially if you study something that requires time, education and money. This is an excellent way to succeed when you are moving to a new country but, more importantly, if you are one of those people that love your profession then this will work for you. As a result, you will find work faster and be able to accommodate your profession.

For example, if you are a doctor, then you can come to Canada first as a student in the medical field. There are a lot of programs, especially in the medical field, where if you study for a Masters' degree in one of the public schools and, if it is in the sciences or medicine, then you can apply directly to the province for permanent residency.

If you have family, your spouse will be able to get an open work permit and your children will be able to attend local schools. I see thousands of immigrants coming over this way, because there are a lot of benefits to it. First, you can get a study permit and work 20 hours per week. After the Master's degree or PhD is completed, you can apply for a post-graduation work permit. More importantly, you can apply as a Permanent Resident for yourself and your family. For your child to come to Canada as an international student, from first grade to grade 12, their tuition ranges from $15,000 thousand per year up to $25,000.00. Right there I can see the benefits of you coming to study, having your spouse working and your children attending school without paying those international fees. This is a great benefit and I have seen a lot of people from all over the world immigrate to Canada for this benefit. However, these rules change constantly and I advise you to get our legal advice prior coming to Canada.

There are also others that love to change or start a completely new life by starting a new program or career. They choose to join the trades industry, such as becoming a plumber, carpenter, electrician, or chef, just to mention a few of them. This provides them with an amazing number of opportunities in a booming economy, where they can be employees of a company for a couple of years. Once they have acquired the necessary working experience, they can open their own business.

There are other successful immigrants that have the mind set of an entrepreneur. These people open their businesses as soon as they arrive. These people understand that they are not required to have a profession or be specialized. They hire people who are specialized or who know the industry or can become their partner. They leverage their time and business knowledge to build wealth with their employees and building strong teams. They surround themselves with smart people.

This is how successful people become well known in their industry, soon after they arrive to this new land full of opportunities. This is why it is important to have a clear picture of what your intention is prior to making the decision to either move to another place permanently or just visit, work or study. It is important that you get the right information. In our company, we provide you with legal advice in immigration matters and also prepare a plan for you according to your needs, prior to you making a decision to immigrate. It is better to make a move with the right information and advice. Our company offers different services; such as legal advice, educational programs, and also provide you access to real estate agents to help you find a place to rent or purchase before you come to this country. We also can assist you in many different languages, such as Spanish, Portuguese, Cantonese, Mandarin, Vietnamese, and Arabic, just to mention a few.

It is important that you also research other information, such as the currency and how long it may take you to upgrade your education to practice your profession in your new country. By researching before making the move, it will help you to see the big picture. Your fear will be lessened. Sometimes fear is lack of knowledge or lack of clarity. But regardless of how you are experiencing the emotion of fear, don't let it stop you.

NEW COUNTRY, NEW BEGINNING

Leave behind everything you don't need when you are coming to a new place, so you are ready to move forward with an open heart to start a new life. If you are single, it is an advantage, because you can choose which culture to marry into; somebody with the same culture or the culture of your new country. Whatever you decide is a great decision, just be open to new relationships. A lot of the new immigrants find this very complex because as I mentioned learning a new culture is very complicated. Other people say that is exactly what they were looking for, a new way of thinking and to find a new start. This is not my experience, but the recollection of thousands of people that I had the opportunity to help either when I was working with the Law Corporate Firm as a Manager of the Immigration Department, or as the CEO of my current company.

If you are coming from a broken marriage, then it is better to stop contacting the friends that you have in common or extended family unless it is necessary, which would be the case if you have children together. However, as soon as your children grow up and have the capacity to communicate directly with their other parent, then allow that to happen. The less contact you have with this other person, the sooner you can move forward and find a new love, if that is what your desire is. No matter where people are coming from, these tips work, because I have had the opportunity to see a lot of women come from their countries, leaving either an abusive or broken marriage. The successful immigrants overcome this situation, and get professional help if they need it. They recognize that they want to live a new life and they are willing to do it, no matter what.

I see women married to the love of their lives and who are happy with them, after they have overcome a separation or abusive marriage. They are open to a new opportunity and are able to find a person that loves them and respects them. Always remember to be open to a new beginning. These people recognize that they can change their lives with these new opportunities; that they can write the next chapter of their lives and so can you, no matter where you are. If you wish to remain in the same country, just move from one city to another, or if you are moving to a new country, you can always choose to have a happy life. It is possible no matter where you are on the planet.

I have also seen people coming here because they are bankrupt, but as soon as they land, they transform this into a new beginning. Soon after, they are out of debt and building a new life. It seems to me that when people are faced with great obstacles and difficulties in their journeys as immigrants but find the strength and discipline to overcome them, the more successful they become in their new country.

If you think you cannot do it, because your problem feels very big and you don't see the new beginning, let me tell you that I see a lot of people coming from all over the world, from such places as Australia, Ireland, England, Mexico, Colombia, Chile, Peru, El Salvador, Guatemala, Vietnam, China, and Hong Kong. No matter where they come from, they all make it happen. It is important to mention that people with less challenges, such as those from Australia, England, or America, don't make a big pivot in their lives. These countries have certain similarities in their cultures, which makes it less of a leap for those immigrants. Remember the more challenges you have before you move, the higher level of success you can reach.

KNOW WHAT YOU ARE GOOD AT

Let us recognize the difference between talent and mission. You may or may not have the talent to complete and fulfill your mission. For example, if you love to sing but you are a terrible singer, then maybe this is a good passion but not a good talent.

You can find what you want while you discover what you

don't want. Are you one of those people that wake up every morning so happy and ready to run to do what you do? Do you wake up way ahead of time and walk the extra mile? Or you are the one that wakes up wishing the day hadn't started? Or do you wake up and show up to work but dislike everything you are doing?

I recalled this phrase as follows: "For the past 33 years, I have looked in the mirror every morning and asked myself, "If today were the last day of my life, would I want to do what I am about to do today? And whenever the answer has been, "No" for too many days in a row, I know I need to change something."

If that is life, then I don't want to live it that way. If I have to wake up and at the end of the day, are doing something that I dislike and does not fulfil my mission, then I would rather not to do it. No matter what the cost is. Remember I told you about having a good job at the government with excellent benefits? I did own a new car and had a good life. I didn't tell you this to brag about myself, but I shared with you my experiences because regardless of how comfortable I was, I was not happy and I didn't want to remain there. I knew I had to make a change in my life, so I took advantage of the changes and I made the decision to leave all that behind in spite of the cost.

But the reward is a life of abundance, happiness, wealth, and health and I give thanks to my God every morning that I wake up. I didn't allow my conditioned mind stop me from moving forward toward my dreams and my plans, even though I was not planning to stay in my adoptive country. I was planning to learn English, then go back and get a scholarship and then return to study for a PhD in sociology. However, the plan changed but not my purpose in life - day by day I get more clarity on my mission and vision in life.

I always love to observe how people react and how people behave in certain circumstances. I recalled as a child always observing people and my own emotions. Many times, I thought this feeling hurts and I don't want to feel it. Later in life, I learned that feelings will always be there, and it is my responsibility to develop the discipline to control them. I observe my feelings and my behaviour and then meditate on why I was allowing someone to control my emotions, or circumstances to control my life. Then I found out that it was my responsibility to decide how I will allow others or circumstances to affect me, so I choose not to let them.

The secret is to remain aware of your emotions and to remain present at all times. Even when you become angry or when certain situations upset you or someone that you don't like shows up, ask yourself why are you allowing this to move your emotions? To make you react?

I wish from the deepest part of my heart that you find what you are good at and step in to your mission. Trust me, there is nothing better than to work at something you enjoy, even if you don't get paid for it. You feel complete and fulfilled. You may tell me, "But I need to eat and buy things and support my family!" I can certainly tell you that you will have that and more. I am telling you that when you quit things that are not fulfilling your mission, you are opening the door of infinitive abundance and will find what you are good at, and along with this comes wealth.

I really hope you take the time and go deep inside yourself. All the wisdom is in you, nowhere else. You can find the answer inside yourself and then the opportunities will appear. You must remain aware of these opportunities.

THINK OUTSIDE THE BOX

Think differently, because there is more out there for you. A lot of people only use the left side of their brain, and forget that they can use the right side of the brain and can awaken their imagination and creativity. This will help to actually solve problems in your work and bring solutions into situations that you could not imagine. The left side of the brain is for reasoning; it is important to use it, but it must be used in conjunction with the right side of the brain, which can unlock all of your creativity and new ideas.

There are so many inventions in the world. I am going to talk about the new ones, like social media. Whether you and I have recognized it or not, we are in the Era of Information, where everyone has access to all the information available. You can Google anything you want and find a lot of information about it. There are plenty of sources available to find anything you want. It is so important to be connected with the world through social media, so that you can offer services and promote your business, especially if used appropriately. What do I mean by this? You can use social media to spend all day looking photos of others, or you use as a tool to get ahead in your business. I believe it is a great tool if used appropriately.

Since we are in the new era, all those who do not learn technology and social media may be forgotten, because they won't be able to work remotely. We can shop online for what we need without having to go to a physical retail store; already we are seeing less and less retail stores, because products can be sold cheaper without the expenses of paying rent, employees and so on. You can have your warehouse and then sell products online and distribute your products from your warehouse (this could be your home). There are a lot of businesses that run this way now, but this is possible only by thinking outside the box and using your creativity, imagination and new life.

The creators of Facebook, Apple and Google, just to mention a few, they thought outside the box. They thought about the needs of the people and created something for them. Who would think that an Apple product would have so much success in their marketing; they create and believe in what they do. This is an example of what I shared earlier; to use the two sides of the brain and implement this into a reality that can bring so much joy and happiness into people's lives and, in addition, create a lot of success when you immigrate to a new country.

FINDING YOUR STRENGTH

Once you have found your passion and/or mission in this world, then you are living in your strength side. The universe will bend to give you anything you need to make your dream a reality. For the universal laws and rules, there is no time and there are no differences. The problem lives in the mind of the human beings that do not believe they dreams can actually become true.

The more I become aware of this, the more I am careful of my thoughts, my life and my emotions. Because I know that with one thought, I can attract everything I want or even more deeply only by wishing. This is why I am connected spiritually with my higher self and the universal laws.

This is why it is very important for you to listen to your heart and intuition; trust me they know better than your conditioned mind. I love to live this way because everything I do is effortless and this way my energy is up all the time, because I don't worry or stress anymore about things. When I wonder about the end result, I go into the gap and do my part by flowing with the universal laws.

I have a big wish and this is the reason why I decided to write this book – because of you. I want to share all this information. I truly want you to be a better person and live in an abundant world.

Dr. Albert Einstein understood these laws and he said, "The most important decision YOU EVER make is whether you believe you LIVE IN A FRIENDLY OR HOSTILE UNIVERSE." The first time I heard this quote, I was in a conference and I realised this to be true. This happened years ago and every time a negative thought came to my mind, I remembered that it was my decision to live and see a friendly universe.

It is all about how you see things. What lens do you see the world with? If you believe you live in a hostile universe, then you do live in a hostile universe, but if you believe you live in a friendly one, then you do live in a friendly universe. Even though sounds repetitive, people still do not understand these universal laws, because if everybody understood this law, we all would be happy, abundant, healthy and wealthy.

I want you to shine and show your highest and brightest potential. I want you to know that no matter who you are, where you are coming from, or what your limitations seem to be, you can achieve anything you want and I mean anything you want. The only limitations you have is yourself and your mindset, because everything you want exists in the universe and it is just waiting for you to believe it from the deepest part of your heart.

With all these years of experience helping people immigrate to Canada, I have developed not only special skills in immigration matters, but also a sensitivity and intuition on how people react in certain circumstances, no matter where they are from. Regardless of education or race or anything else, people respond similarly in certain situations.

The rich make money easily and effortlessly, which I truly believe is a skill we all can learn. We all can learn how to be connected with our highest selves and let the universe conspire with us to have a life of abundance that you won't even regret for a minute. My major wish is that you become a successful immigrant as I am and that you live a life of abundance in a friendly universe where everything can be right, full of peace, love, health and money.

You can go anywhere you want, buy anything you want and then wait and see that money keeps coming your way in the highest amounts and effortlessly. This will help you to have a wonderful life. More importantly, then and only then, you can help others in a massive way to impact their lives as well.

The more you help others, the more the universe bends over to help you. The key is to remain present and aware. Have intentions written down and follow through. Schedule your activities every day in your calendar; remember to schedule time for yourself and what is important for you. The end result should be that you have only things that you enjoy in your calendar. But you can start by making small changes daily that can have a big impact in your life.

To set a clear example, if you love to exercise but your excuse is that you cannot make it because you are so busy at work or with your family. Then you are forgetting the most important person on this planet is you. You are such a beautiful and magnificent creature; so special that no one can be like you, and if you only believe this, you will have everything you want in life. Please start with scheduling an activity for one hour to do anything you would like to do. Now you can tell me, I cannot do it because I love to play golf and I don't have the money to pay for the golf course and weekly lessons. Then I will suggest you find a friend that does have the resources and accessibility to do it. Propose to this person that you will come to play with them and in exchange, you will help for them with anything they need for one hour. There are a lot of people that love to play golf, who would love to have someone available to play with them or help them while they play. This way you will trick your mind and soon enough the resources will show up for you to have the money and the time. Anything you can think that you might want is possible. Remember the impossible only lives in your mind.

CHAPTER 6

IT IS NEVER TOO LATE TO START
YOUR IMMIGRATION PROCESS

LIVING WITHOUT STATUS

I F YOU ARE IN A new country without any status - whether you are in the USA, Canada or any other country, I believe that you should look for professional legal advice to find out what the possibilities are for you to get legal status in that country. I meet a lot of people, not only in Canada but also in the USA, that are without status. These people live with a lot of fear and limitations; some of them haven't seen their families for years. I cannot imagine families separated because of borders or because one of the family members has to come another country and the rest of the family must stay in their home country. This is the history of a lot of people in America and Canada. However, in Canada, there are certain rules and laws that can allow you to get legal status if you meet certain requirements.

There are some people that come to my office after many years of being without status in the country. I study their cases, give them solutions, and we fix their problems inside the country and get them their permanent residency. I even tell them, if they had come to see me before, I would have gotten them papers a long time ago. These people live in a country without any rights in any sense. They live in the country like it is a jail, unable to travel back and forth from one place to another. At least the USA allows the children of people who have no legal status to attend school until Grade 12. In Canada, it is more complicated than that.

In Canada, no one can attend school unless their parents have status in the country. If in the case of a child that is required to attend school and is at the primary, secondary or high school level, they won't be able to attend school unless the parents have status or another person has custody of this child. This is only the case if the child was born in Canada. If the child was not born in Canada, then the laws will require you to apply for a study visa and you will be charged international fees. Let's illustrate this with an example.

A family is living in Canada without status; they entered years ago, lost their status and remained illegally in the country. Years later, this couple decided to start a family and they have a child in Canada; thus, the child is born Canadian. This does not give the parents legal status automatically. It could help in certain cases, but not always. Also, the mother of this Canadian born child has a sister who is a Canadian citizen. When the child has grown to 5 years old, the child will need to be enrolled in school. The parents of this child will need to give custody of the child to the aunt (or any other relative or friend) so that this child could attend school. Now not all the districts or school boards will accept this. There are some districts that are stricter than others. This child could potentially attend school, but under the custody of another person who has status in Canada. However, imagine that the same family arrived to Canada when their children were only 1 year old and another one was 3 years old. This family does not worry about anything, and loses their status. The family just forgot to ask for legal advice. Once the child reaches the age of 5 years old, this family starts having problems because they cannot enroll their child into school unless the child has an international student visa and custody is assigned again to a family member or friends. Like I explained in my previous chapters, the schooling costs for international students ranges from $15,000 to up to $25,000 per year. This is a lot of money for a family that does not have legal status in the country.

There are several situations when people just overstay and they do not seek legal advice until one of the following happens:

1. The children cannot attend school.

2. They get detained by the police for a traffic violation.

3. They are in the hospital due to a serious illness or an accident.

Sometime it is too late for me to help them. If they had come to my office just before one of the above happened, I could have potentially helped them. This is does not mean that this happened to them and we are unable to do anything for them. What it is means is that we may not be able to do anything for them inside Canada, but we could do more after they have been removed from Canada if we apply to the Canadian embassy overseas. If you need legal advice regarding your status in Canada, please reach out to me at www.canadaimmigrate.ca.

ALWAYS REMEMBER THAT YOU ARE IN A NEW COUNTRY WITH NEW RULES

If you don't know what is happening with your case or situation, find legal advice from professionals, either consultants or lawyers in Canada. These people would be able to help you to clarify your immigration legal questions or to tell you what your best options are. Don't listen to people that have no idea on the subject. First, there are a lot of people that come to see me and I ask them, "Why you didn't come in before?" Their answer is because my friend or relative told me that I don't have to worry and I could just stay. What happens is that people lose a lot of opportunities regarding their immigration legal status. In our company, LSF Immigration Consultants, we not only provide you personalized immigration legal advice, but we are also help you to create a successful map to succeed in Canada. This is why it is important to contact us once you arrive in Canada or prior coming to Canada. This rule will apply if you are interested in moving to any other country as well. As soon as you land in the new country, find legal advice about benefits of studying, how to obtain a work permit, what is the maximum time you are allowed to remain in the country, and so on.

Remember that being unaware of the rules and laws does not mean that you are allowed to break them. Not even if you unintentionally break them. There are consequences for this and it could be devastating for a lot of cases.

CHOOSING LEGAL OR MEDICAL ADVICE

We must carefully choose the person who will help us to achieve our mission and vision when it comes to immigration matters. First, ask your friends and family, or inquire at community centers to find out if they know of anyone who they could recommend. Once you have a few names, Google them and find out as much as you can about them. Usually for me to choose an accountant or doctor, I have to only look at their photo profile on their website to make a decision of whether I can trust that person or not. But remember, I have developed my senses deeply enough that I can do it without error now. So I suggest you to take a first consultation, even if you have to pay for it and hear different opinions. Stay with the person that inspires your trust, and gives you a better plan.

Quite often I have clients come in and complain about the jobs that other professionals have done. Then they tell me that their friend did it that way, and the friend achieved positive results, which is why they hired the same professional advisor. However, I always tell them every case is different and I study each case on its own merits. It is not like we have a system that if you answer all my questions correctly, then you can apply and whoever does not answer them correctly, then they do not qualify.

Just verify the years of experience the professional has. How many cases has this person handled with certain similarities to yours, and what is the rate of success overall? Once you have chosen the right professional, then go and do everything this professional tells you to do and trust the process.

Throughout this book, I have been teaching you about the power of success. A lot of people attract their own failure, even when it comes to legal matters. You may get scared and say, "How this could be, Linda? I don't believe you." Well, I can tell you that some people live naturally under stress and with a lot of negativity. I get my client a work permit that is linked with an employer. This means they can only work for this employer, under the position that the government is indicating and only in that location. For whatever reason, these people lose their jobs; perhaps they got fired, or the company went bankrupt. They end up without a job and are unable to work legally with other employers because they have to change their work permit to be with another sponsor (employer). Needless to say, these people try to find another sponsor and they cannot find someone. Soon they do not have legal status. They either hide in the country or they return to their home country, and it is all because of their mindset and negativity. They stress so much that they cannot even trust themselves; so how can they trust their legal counsel? I explain to them the processing times and how long it will take, but they call every week to find out when they are getting their immigration answer.

After over a decade of experience in serving immigrants, I know how they will react during the whole process. Remember I started by saying that you must choose your legal counsel and hire the one that makes you feel comfortable and that you can trust, because only by trusting them will they help you in your own profession. Honestly, I would rather you not hire me to do your immigration papers than deal with a person that suffers from anxiety. I am sorry I am telling you this, but it is a reality. You need to start trusting that the universe can handle your deepest wishes and the intentions of your heart. The universal laws and the spiritual connection is more powerful than anything.

One of my mentors, Deepak Chopra, says in one of his books, "You must learn to live without attachments to be free." What do I mean by this? Well, you must learn to live with a planner in your hand, but be able to change the routes every time life requests it. I don't know if you have ever lived in a situation where you are so mad because of the traffic, or you are so mad because they didn't sell you the house you wanted, or they fired you from your work or you got divorced.

You only see the blessing after time passes and you think, now I understand why this all happened to me. It was only to protect me or it was working in my favor. You don't see it at the time, but trust me, there is a reason for everything. The universal laws are powerful and smarter than you and I put together. Trust in the process, whether it is a legal situation, medical problem or any other problem that you are facing or waiting to resolve. Believe me that I have taken the journey and that is why I am writing this book, because I want you to live an abundant life, and this means freedom for your mind, heart, finances, health and relationships with others.

Credibility is very important when it comes to finding a legal representative for your immigration matters. Look into their past cases and if more than one person has recommended the same services over and over again. Then that person has built a reputation of credibility. In my company, we have a rule, and I say rule because we are a team that function together like the organs in a body, that we all have a role but we are always putting our best self forward. When we decide to take your case, but also if we decide not to take your case for any reason, we will send you with someone that we trust and believe can provide you the services you deserve in your case. We have had some cases when we believed we could not take the case because it is outside of our expertise, but we always send you to the right place where they can help. My company is growing and will continue growing and the reason this happens is because I do have credibility with my clients. They either had a recommendation or they believed in me as soon as they met me.

FOLLOW THE ADVICE AND TAKE THE RISK

Once you have chosen the right legal counsel, then please take their advice and move forward. Don't say, "I will think about it", and then come back in 30 days. The longer you wait, the closer you are to the risk of never getting it done until you are in trouble, as I mentioned previously.

I truly advise you that as soon as you find your legal advisor, sign that same day. If you cannot pay your retainer that day, then make an arrangement to come back that week with the retainer. I am not suggesting you to go the first appointment you have and sign a retainer agreement, but I am suggesting you do it once you have done your research to find your legal counsel. A lot of people wait so long to take action in things that are important for their immigration, and the same goes for everything else they do in their lives.

Take action when your heart and intuition direct you to do so. Just as you learned basic skills like writing and reading, I would like you to develop another basic skill; listening to your intuition and your heart, and paying close attention to them.

TURNING A NEGATIVE INTO A POSITIVE

I have been repeating a lot that if you remain present and aware, then you can have a beautiful life. You have been created with a lot of potential. You are intelligent, perfect, and unique - there is no one like you in the whole universe. This is how perfect this creation is; there is no one like you now, and there never will be and there never has been someone like you. This is why, no matter where you are living, if you do not have legal status in the country, then you are turning that positive into a negative. However, if you do what you need to do, then you turn all that negative into a positive and set your intentions on getting it right this time. The universe does not exist in the past and will not exist in the future. If you are blaming yourself for the past mistakes you have made and for the wrong decisions you have made, you won't solve anything. Your immigration status will remain unchanged and your regret won't change anything in your life. However, if you move forward and act in the present time, you will turn all those negative decisions in the past into positive ones. Then you will be able to make a way to change your situation.

This works in any area of your life - trust me, ANY area of your life. If you think positive and remain positive regardless of the circumstances you are living in, soon enough your energy will transform and you will be attracting positive things to your life. The people that come to you will be positive, the resolutions you are waiting for will be positive and suddenly, all the people around you will be positive.

DIFFERENT RULES, DIFFERENT AREAS

There are different rules for every area that you wish to apply for during your process to come to Canada. To start in Canada, we have a federal law and a provincial law. Both of these areas are different.

There are several programs under the federal laws, I will just list a few of them:

1. Express Entry
    a. Skilled workers

   b. Trades

   c. Canadian Experiences Class

2. The Family Are:

   a. Sponsoring parents and grandparents

   b. Sponsoring the dependent children

   c. Sponsoring spouses or common law partners in land

   d. Sponsoring spouses of common law partners outside Canada

3. Investor programs at the federal level (This is a closed door for now because you must prove that you have a net worth of 10 million dollars and that you will invest 2 million with the risk of losing your money, because there are no guarantees at this time.)

There are also programs specific to each of the provinces.

1. British Columbia

2. Alberta

3. Ontario

4. Nova Scotia

5. New Brunswick

Most of these provinces have programs for Skilled Workers, semi-skilled workers (only in a few provinces), and investors (good programs for investors in the provinces). For example, in British Columbia, we have a program where you must prove that your net worth is $600,000 and that you are ready to invest $200,000 in a business in B.C. There is another program in the province of New Brunswick where you must have a $400,000 net worth and be willing to invest $125,000 in a business, and leave a deposit of $75,000 if the business plan does not get implemented as you proposed. The province will keep your deposit, but you get to stay in the country versus the provinces of B.C. and Ontario, where if you don't meet the conditions of the business plan, then you won't get the nomination certificate and they can return you back to your country. It will depend on what you want to have and where you want to settle.

CHAPTER 7

WAYS TO GET A HOME IMMEDIATELY

NOW THAT YOU HAVE ENTERED your new country and you have solved your legal situation, you are ready to settle in. The second important thing you must focus your energy on is getting a home. First, because the more rent you are paying the more money you are wasting, instead of paying on your mortgage for your house.

This is why as soon as you know that you are able to stay in your new country permanently, start looking for a house or apartment. How can you find a place that is suitable for you? I am not a real estate agent, but I am an active investor who is always searching for deals and looking for ways to invest my money and get a high return. I love real estate. I love to put my money in real estate - the reason being that it is a tangible investment that I can see and have.

Below are the tips that I use myself to find the right investment for me:

1. The first tip is the first money that I will make is going to be on the purchase price, so I search for

houses or properties where I can negotiate prices. For example, people that are rushing to sell due to divorce matters, wills, leaving the country, or even those people that just want to sell to move to a new property. These sellers are usually motivated to sell, because they either want to get out of trouble or they are interested in just moving out of their home. These are a good target because they are open to negotiating the prices of their properties. If you notice I did not mention people who are ill; the reason why I didn't mention this is because I will never try to get a house at a lower market value when a family member is ill. I will actually pay the market price if I am interested in other benefits of the property that I will mention below. The rest of the circumstances are acceptable when someone wants to divorce and they need to divide the house. Families in this cases are willing to negotiate the price.

2. The second tip is looking at the potential of the property to increase in value. For example, maybe today the surrounding area is a not developed town, but in a few years, that city will be developed. The benefits will be in the increased value of my property. In this situation, I will get the property. Another example is purchasing an apartment for $120,000. I can rent it for $600 a month, creating a cash flow. At the same time, the equity of the property will increase to $300,000 within the next three to five years. As you can see, it does not matter if I paid full price, because I pocket some money through the rental and my investment tripled in the next few years. This is a great way to buy a property.

3. The third circumstance is to consider the purchase in pre-sell as part of a construction project. I always will end up with a better price - I will purchase at

the lower price, and usually these properties increase in value as soon as they finish the construction of the development. Because usually there is not only the construction of the building, but there is the development of certain businesses and this increases the value of my property.

4. The fourth tip is very important - if you are buying this property to live in yourself, look for one that can provide you with extra income, typically by renting out the basement. At the same time that you purchase your home, you can start making income that helps to cover your mortgage. This tip is very helpful especially if you have the money for the down payment and the bank or the institution that lends you the money will approve your investment. Then it is a good opportunity to get a bigger place than an apartment. An apartment usually has something called strata fees, so you always have to pay these fees to maintain the building. If you are only getting this property for investment purposes and you do not plan to live in this property, then watch for the best place with the lowest strata fee. Some apartments have a pool and a gym and this increases the strata fee. So if you are looking to purchase a property that is only for rent, find places that do not have pool or gym to keep your monthly expenses down, thus allowing you to keep more of the rental income.

Also, it is important to see the rules in the apartment building, because there are some conditions that do not allow owners to rent the place, others are only for specific ages, and others do not allow pets. You want to look specifically for those conditions and make your decision according to the situation. For example, a place that only allows elderly people to live there is a great option for you to invest in first, because you will always have someone to rent your place at a reasonable price. Usually all retired people have a pension that they receive every month from the government or their private pensions.

GETTING CREDIT

Credit is actually easier to obtain for applicants when they are newcomers. The banks provide them more opportunities to get their new home. This will make it easier for you to get your loan, especially if you are working under payroll and have the 20 percent for the down payment. It is in your best interest to have this percentage, because you won't have to pay more interest and additional fees for mortgage insurance.

The other tip to really get a loan is to apply for a credit card as soon as you get into the country and always pay your credit payment on time. Every month you should pay off the credit card, and also try to purchase furniture or things establish yourself in the new country, especially if we are talking about Canada.

Get a loan or credit for a car or other necessary things. More importantly, budget yourself to save. The more money you can save, the less interest you pay. The best credit is where you get the lowest interest rate possible.

OPPORTUNITIES FOR NEWCOMERS

How do you see yourself - as a newcomer with a lot of opportunities or a person who lacks personality and opportunities in life? Because whatever you believe, that is exactly what is going to happen with your life. If you believe this new country has a lot of opportunities for you, then the country will have it. If you believe there are no opportunities for you, then there won't be. I won't argue this with you because you are the only one who can change this situation.

Opportunities are all around us, all the time - the question is, do you see these opportunities around you? Are you aware of these opportunities? Are you open to new opportunities? Are you willing to change and move out of your comfort zone? If the answer is yes, then start looking for all these opportunities around you, and take advantage of those opportunities, no matter how much fear you may be feeling. Trust me, if you take the step to move forward, you will take the ride of the new opportunity and then enjoy the beauty.

Please open your mind and expand your opportunities - call the new opportunities to your life with your mind. One of my mentors, Bob Proctor, has a big saying that follows, "If you can hold it in your mind, you can hold it in your hands." It so true - you can imagine any opportunity in your mind, first within your imagination, then the subconscious mind kicks in and starts creating and converting it into reality. Believe it and know this is a science and this works in life. There are no more limits but those in your mind.

You have to see yourself as a person full of opportunities. Previously I spoke about the importance of being aware and remaining present at all times. There are opportunities that can pass to you and you are not able to see them. Then those opportunities pass and you are complaining that there are no opportunities for immigrants. If there are no opportunities for me, then I will create the opportunities, because I try to have clarity before I move forward. Once I know what I want, I will do what it takes to make that happen.

APPLYING CREDIT SCORE STRATEGIES LEGALLY

I touched a bit on this topic before about credit scores. The way you increase your credit score is not by using your credit card to buy clothes, shoes, food and all those needs. A lot of people use them now because credit cards give you points or flights the more you shop with them. But in reality to increase your credit score, you need to buy things that are important. For example, getting a house or making a down payment for the deposit of the house or apartment you wish to buy, and opening a new business are good ways to use credit wisely. Actual things that will give you revenue as time passes.

The credit score looks at what you spend your money on. If you spend all your salary on shopping, clothes, and trips, then they will see you as a person that spend a lot of money frivolously. It is hard to believe that this person will be reliable with their finances when it comes to getting a loan for a house. Banks can lend you the money you want to buy a house or an apartment, but I want you to see the difference between one thing and another. I want you to see that the credit department will give you a higher amount of credit if you are not spending all your money on clothing, material items, dinner or things that won't create credit for you.

Money exists on a different level that is spiritual. Of course, representation in this life at a physical level is currency, whether it is dollars or pesos. Look at the meaning of money in the dictionary. It is defined as follows: "Something (such as coins or bills) used as a way to pay for goods and services and to pay people for their work." So it is an exchange of services that you provide to the public. If you are offering a service to serve a majority of the population, you will get more money and this will be a window to many opportunities. As much as you are serving, means that much more money that you will earn.

Keep in mind that you are the creator of the opportunities that you have. If you are not satisfied with your results, it is because you are not calling the right opportunities that you want. It is time for you to step in and be the director of your own movie and begin directing your life and your wishes.

GET SPECIALIZED

Always be specialized in whatever you are doing. In the proportion that you provide the service, that will be the same proportion that you will make money from it. Focus on becoming specialized, but remember, YOU do not need to be specialized! You can be the CEO of your company, but you find yourself specialized people for each of the positions that are required in your company. For example, if you have an accounting department or a legal department, you hire people who are specialized in those areas, because in this way you will be able to provide high end services.

It is very important that you understand that you do not need to be specialized, and you may not be able to be specialized in all the areas of your company, because that would be difficult. No one can be specialized in all areas. It is important for you to provide services, but to surrender yourself with those who are specialized.

The same works for people that have a design company. They won't be able to have expertise in all areas of the company. They can have a designer, an architect, a painter and more, with all of them able to provide the necessary specialized services.

This is how the rich become richer and the poor become poorer. There are a lot of professionals that are barely able to survive because they have in their minds that they are irreplaceable, that they need to see all the clients, and that they need to do all the work because there is no one that can do the work as well as they can do it. Well, they are called self-employed, because if you are required to work in your business more than 20 hours per week, then you have no business; you are self-employed. This is where you create the job and then do it yourself or review everyone and do the job again. A real business that is specialized creates systems and the owners surrender themselves to people that are specialized in this type of work. The owners of the business have implemented such great systems that their business can run without the owner being there more than 20 hours per week.

BECOME AN EXCELLENT MONEY MANAGER

You can develop the ability to invest your money, and let your money work hard for you instead of you working for your money. You are one step away from becoming financially free.

I understand that for some of you this is a new way of thinking because we haven't been taught this at school for 12 years, if we count grade 1 to grade 12.

It is important that you become a good manager and if your money arrives to you, it is your responsibility to make that money grow and make more money. Like I mentioned in previous chapters, you can invest your money in real estate but you also can invest your money in the stock market, in other businesses, in ideas and so on. There are several ways that you can make your money work hard for you and grow.

You are responsible for converting those pennies that you earn into dollars and then those dollars into thousands and those thousands into millions. I won't tell you that this is easy since you have been raised with a lot of paradigms about money. I have been raised myself with a lot of limitations. In my experience, my parents didn't like to spend any money on anything. They did live with limits and saved almost everything; there were no holidays for the family. We could not eat at restaurants or wear any fancy or expensive clothes. On the other hand, regardless of their limited education, they managed to build a fair amount of wealth in their later ages. I grew up with this, so as soon as I could I started earning money, which was in a very young age. I always managed to sell something at school, outside on the streets and so on. I manage to buy what I wanted. When I began working for the government and making money, I managed to earn money and spend all the money I earned and more on everything. I wanted, holidays, clothes, you name it, I bought it. This created a cycle; the more I earned, the more I spent. I just managed to make all that money disappear.

Later in life I wondered why? Why do I manage to spend all my money? And soon I realized, by studying and reading and meditating, that I didn't know what to do with it. Nobody at school taught me that my money could work hard for me and make me more and more money instead of me just working. I did not have any other file in my mind besides go find a job and work and make money and spend money. Once I realized

I could make my money work for me, I began my own business and began building my own wealth. However, is it this easy? The answer is no; sometimes I forgot and went on a spending spree. Why does this happen? Because the conditioned mind is in between and wants to get me back into my old habits and not move forward.

I must remind myself actively that I have a budget for anything I want. If I want to buy any clothes or shoes or anything, first I must make an investment and make my business work for me. I have created conditions in my mind that investing comes first, then shopping.

This is a great way to learn how to use your money, change your habits and apply new ideas into your mind and your life. Trust me, you will end up having a more significant life when there is meaning in the things you do, instead of having a life driven by emotions you don't know how to handle or don't want to even realize you have them.

I have created a coaching program for you to see things differently financially, and learn how to manage your money to create more wealth. Soon enough you will find yourself doing what you love the most, whatever it is you love to do, whether that be playing golf, tennis, writing a book, or travelling. You can do anything because you will have the money and the time. If you want to learn more about my exciting programs, I invite you to continue into the next chapter because I guarantee you that what you will learn is invaluable in terms of both time and money.

CHAPTER 8

BUDGETING TO BECOME FINANCIALLY FREE

I EXPLAINED HOW TO MANAGE YOUR money in the previous chapter. Now I am going to show you step by step how to become financially free as soon as you can. This can be done in two years or less. Yes, in two years or less! How can this happen, you ask? Well, very easy – by reducing your expenses every month, and finding more meaning in your life.

1. You need to verify all your expenses to determine what you are spending every month. When I started to figure out how much money I was spending, I opened an Excel page and then wrote down every penny that was leaving my pocket, whether it was necessary or not. If it was necessary, then I said yes. But if I was overspending on things that were wants, then I said no and it reduced my expenses. I found out that I didn't need to have two cars, but only one. By selling one, I saved over $500 every month between insurance, gas and maintenance on

my car. I also started to pack my lunch and my food for my day, which helped me with my saving, but also with my health. I lost weight and got in shape. Is this important to you? Well this is the way you can do it. You pack your lunch from home, and you become healthy. I also got rid of my nanny and saved over $1,000 dollars. I started watching my monthly grooming expenses, such as hair, nails, and so on, which usually I spent over $300 per month on. Once I saw where I was spending money, I adjusted. My relationship with money became healthier, so more money came to me.

2. You must create an Excel page that lists all your expenses and all your sources of income, so you can see how you are spending your money and ways to increase your income. This is a very important topic because you need to believe that you deserve more money. If you are an employee and you want to get an increase in your salary, what are you going to do to make it happen? Are you going to become more efficient in your position? What do you need to do to make yourself the person who deserves an increase in salary? A lot of people want an increase in salary and believe they deserve it, but they are not giving 100 percent of themselves in their jobs or position so they are getting paid accordingly. Do you give 100 percent in what you do? Do you provide your best service in whatever you do? Do you walk the extra mile in everything you do? Are you passionate about what you do? Does time fly when you are doing your work? Do you see yourself as worthy? If the answer is yes, then meet with your boss and ask for an increase in your salary. Your manager will tell you the answer as soon as you step in front of them. Also, you must be prepared with a plan to explain why you deserve

this increase, how much your increase should be, and why the company should give it to you. You need to make them see the benefits, not just for you, but for the company. Show them the benefits of having a great employee like you continue working in their company.

If you own a business and want to make $1,000,000 dollars in one year or every six months, then create a clear idea that you will get this money in that time frame. How much should the prices for your services increase for you to reach your goal? Also, it is vital to have the reasons why do you deserve to sell $1,000,000 versus your competitors. Finally, what are you going to do with this money? It does not matter if you tell me that you will spend it on the car of your dreams, trips, or anything else you want - all the reasons are valid as long as you are sure of them.

BUDGETING THE FIRST TWO YEARS

Unless you are a millionaire already, you must budget for the first two years after you land in the new country. If you would never travel outside your country but you wish to change your finances, this is also an important step for you. It does not matter whether you like to travel or not, the most important factor is that you budget for the next two years. What do I mean by this? Well, you created a list of expenses and a list of income and have looked for ways to decrease the expenses and increase the income. Only by doing this you will be able to create wealth. If you are in debt already, do not add to this debt by putting one more penny on your credit card. Consider getting a second job and devoting all the earnings to exclusively pay off your debts.

Focus on reducing debts that you have and reducing all your expenses. Remember fancy cars are not an investment. If you have multiple car payments, can you reduce them by reducing the number of cars you own?

Once you have gotten out of debt, continue living the same lifestyle. Don't start spending but instead, take the amount you were spending on your debt payments to the bank. Do this for the same amount of time that it took you to get out of debt. If it took you one year to get out of debt, then for one year you will be saving the same amount of money as you just paid off. This savings is now going to be used strictly for investments.

What can you invest the money in? Well, if you are a person who provides a professional service but are an employee to a governmental institution, then you can start your own business - at the beginning only part-time. You have saved the money that can help you to rent an office and to hire a secretary to answer your phone and book appointments. If you are lawyer, and work during the day with the government, then you can have your private consultation law, where you can provide services in the evenings or afternoons. Then invest the money that this practice brings to you. You won't touch the money for another 2 years. You can hire other lawyers that can provide consultation in other areas outside of your speciality. If you are a criminal lawyer, then you hire someone who specializes as a labour lawyer or civil lawyer. Then you have other people working for you and making money for you. When the two years has ended, you can decide if you want to continue working for the employer you have or you go and run your own company full-time. A lot of the people I know decided to be the owners of their own business. How long will it take for you to become financially free? Two sets of two years, and this is if you are in debt. Some of my clients are ahead of the game and do not have any debts and instead of that they saved. These people can be financially free in two years.

I know you are still wondering, how do I become financially free? I just quit my job and now I have to start running my own company? Yes, that is true, but there are differences between running your own company and being an employee. Now even if you don't show up to the company, the other lawyers you have hired will still generate money for you. Do you see the difference? First, if you didn't wake up in the morning to go and work you didn't get paid, and they could even fire you from your job. Now you are the owner of the business, so you can either wake up or not and you can also make your own schedule. Let us say that you love to pick your children up from school and have dinner with them; so now you can do that by not scheduling any clients during this time. Let us say that you love to go and play golf twice per week, so you create your work schedule around those times.

You could hire more lawyers so you don't have to do all the work. You have the brand and the name, but others will do it for you. The same math works for doctors, mechanics, carpenters, architects, designers and even cleaners or any other profession or office. There is no excuse for you to not become financially free.

MAKE IT A HABIT

This is another piece of the puzzle. If you have good habits, then you will become financially free. Believe me, if you apply my previous advice, then you will. I have helped thousands of people to become financially free and very successful, not only by coming to Canada, but also by applying these principles that make them successful. I coach them and help them to implement these new habits into their lives. It is all about habits. If you are unable to break the old habits, you won't be able to win this race because of the paradigms still living in your subconscious mind. Only by creating new actions and turning them into habits can you achieve all the dreams that your heart desires. Otherwise, they are only wishes that never become a reality.

There is nothing that makes me happier than having people succeeding in their lives. Seeing people become financially free with a strong intention on changing their habits.

Trust me, small changes can create big results in the future. The more you implement all those habits that I just taught you, the more money and financial freedom you can have. Then, and only then, you can get anything you want - like cars, houses, and trips. You can even help others in massive ways that will impact their lives.

The only way you will break a habit is by repetition and by constantly doing what you say you will do. Then even if you fail and remember we all fail and it is ok to fail, there is nothing wrong with it. However, if you fail, then you need to get back on track and continue to work on your plan. Repeat the process, you will see that energy will flow and you will start automatically doing the new habit you have created. Some books teach you that you require 90 days to break a habit. For me, it took longer and I continue watching myself constantly for signs that I am slipping back into my old habits. I watch my habits, my actions, my thoughts, and my behavior because I want to break my old paradigms and make them into wins in my life and the lives of others. Is this process easy? No, but is this process worth it? YES, without a doubt! I can tell you that this process is absolutely worth it. After implementing this into my life, I have seen dramatic changes and it has given me freedom.

HOW DOES THIS MAKE A DIFFERENCE IN YOUR LIFE?

Massively changing your life will cause changes in all aspects; your vision will increase, your intuition will increase, and the possibilities for you to create opportunities will increase in such a way that literately you will see opportunities everywhere you go.

As your imagination gets expanded, you will be able to increase your income, your business and your quality of life in an amazing way that you can't put a price on. You will also grow spiritually because ABUNDANCE comes in all forms: wealth, health, happiness and freedom. You will have a complete life in all aspects of your life. You will create better relationships with your partner, children, parents, friends, and employees. They will want to be with you and learn more and more from you.

They will wish to become like you and help you to achieve your dreams. Imagine a partner that says to you, "That is an amazing idea, what can I do to help you?" Or an employee telling you, "I will do my best to turn your idea into reality because only together we can achieve massive results."

Your health will be at 100 percent. You will be feeling more energetic and happier. It does not matter what age you are, you will be able to achieve anything. I have clients that at the age of 60 run marathons that they could never do at the age of 30. Is this telling you something? I believe so, if your energy is channeled in the right direction, then you end up with more energy and more happiness, and more fulfillment with a sense of the mission in your life.

I spoke to you about the mission in your life and how important this is in the life of every human being. Because we all have been sent to this planet with a mission, but we forgot about it and condition ourselves and our minds with our culture, languages, family traditions and so on. This is why coming to a multicultural country is a win for you, because you can break free from all those paradigms that you have. You can have an open mind to so many other languages, learn about so many new traditions or religions, and see a diversity of cultures and families.

By observing other people from different cultures, you will become more open-minded and start thinking outside the box. Now you can see the creation on the planet is bigger and has so much diversity. When you are able to expand your mind with this and gain the ability to learn from those cultures, you win. Then you are able to create magic in your life.

We all should be able to live in a place of harmony, peace, and abundance in all aspects, but unfortunately, you don't live in this world because you don't believe this is possible. You need to believe you can live in Utopia, and trust me you can live in Utopia - I live there and this is where magic happens. I invite you to get on the ride and see life from here. Trust me, the perspective from here is beautiful, magical, and is a song that you can enjoy singing. It is waking up every morning full of grace and feeling grateful to God for everything and anything you have. Because certainly not everything in life is about money. When I started this book, I first spoke about your mission and finding out what makes you happy. What do you love to do on this planet? Because when you find it, then you will find the land of Utopia that I guarantee you is fun and an amazing way to live in ABUNDANCE.

Here is only gratitude, peace, love, fun, and the most amazing feeling that all human beings should experience in life.

WHERE YOU SHOULD PUT YOUR MONEY

I have investors from all over the world wishing to come to Canada under the investor programs. They ask me, where do you think is the best place to invest my money? What type of business? A lot of people come to me asking me the same questions. I always analyse the background of the person and explain to them what the best way is for them.

Let us say that you are an owner of a restaurant in your country; then I invite you to invest your money in restaurants. You may ask, why in restaurants? First, because you know the industry better, so you have less of a chance of failing if you already know the industry. If you are coming to this country and do not want to work in the same industry that you are working in now, then the best option for you is to buy a franchise because they already own a system that will work with or without your direct input. You make the investment in the franchise and what you are really buying is the system that they have. For example, McDonalds, Starbucks, Taco Bell and so on are all businesses that are franchises. The name and the system are key. More importantly, they will be continuously advertising for the company and creating new menus, so you can continue bringing new stuff to customers. Yes, a franchise is an expensive investment, but they come with a guaranteed return, especially because of the recognised name. I will advise you to get one if you can afford to buy it. You will generate income with little or no work in the place because you can hire managers to manage the business and run it for you.

Another place to invest your money is in pre-existing businesses where their owners are looking to retire. They are selling their business because they no longer want to run it. These are usually small businesses, but a very profitable way to start in a new country. The reason is that you buy the business and it already has clients, many of which they have had for years. If you continue providing the same level of customer service, products and pricing, these clients will keep coming back. In addition, you bring on new products or services that the customers will love and you are able to expand the business. This is the one of the best ways to invest your money in a pre-existing business that you wish to run.

Another way to invest your money that I love is real estate, because as I explained before, this way you make money on the investment in two ways, through rental cash flow and the increasing value of the property itself. This is an excellent way of investment if you buy at a good price and you can hold it for the long term.

GETTING CASH FLOW

This is my favorite topic because for years, I lived without it. It is so much fun collecting money without any effort, and knowing that this cash flow can pay for your living expenses or for your trips or any luxuries that you want. When do you buy the BMW you want? When you have enough cash flow coming every month to pay the monthly installments for the car, so you don't work for it, because others will work for it and you will enjoy the fun of it.

The second way of earning cash flow is to become part of a network marketing system that has a great product to offer to others, and you can make money from it. For example, If you join AMWAY, it would not only help you to develop yourself personally, but also it would provide a great product for you to offer in the market. If you follow the steps to create the system and have other people offering the products for you, then you can create cash flow. The more you do it, the more you earn and then you can create cash flow without even working yourself. There are a lot of companies that offer the opportunity to become a promoter if you want to go this way. Search for a good product and a great company to help you to develop yourself as a professional and as a person in all aspects.

CHAPTER 9

KNOW WHICH INSTITUTIONS CAN GIVE YOU SUPPORT

For more information check my website,
MYSUCCESSFULIMMIGRANT.COM.

GETTING YOUR DRIVER'S LICENSE

GETTING YOUR DRIVER LICENSE IS bit more complex in Canada than in other countries. This is true even if you already know how to drive, especially if you are coming from countries like Asia, Latin America, South America, and Central America, to mention a few. I suggest you take a few classes with a driving school that will show you the routes and places that you will be driving during your test. This will help you to pass the test the first time. There are a lot of benefits that these classes can provide you with. They will give you tips on how to drive, what to do and the things the officers are reviewing when you are taking the driving test.

Below are a few schools that I suggest you contact before you take the driving test:

- All Seasons Driving School
- Best Choice Driving School

- Driving Guru Training Institute Inc.
- Durham's Elite Driving School Inc.

This is just a few of them, but if you wish to find more driving schools, visit the link below.
http://www.mto.gov.on.ca/english/driver/driving-schools.shtml#b.

Another tip is to get a letter from the insurance company in your country where you have driven previously, which includes your driving record. If your records prove that you have never had an accident before it will help you to reduce the cost of your car insurance. In addition, I advise you to have your driver's license and that you take it with you to the translations. They can authorize the time you drove in your country and consider it for your Canadian license.

OTHER INSTITUTIONS

Schools that are authorized by the government of Canada if you wish to apply for Study Visa.

Name of School	Number	City
AAA Aviation Flight Academy	O110735702489	Langley
Academy of Classical Oriental Sciences (ACOS)	O19256958102	Nelson
Academy of Learning College	O212477056057	Abbotsford
Academy of Learning College	O212477063807	Langley
Academy of Learning College -	O19395300024	Victoria

Academy of Learning College	O110096211204	Richmond
Academy of Learning College	O19361063652	Surrey
Academy of Learning College	O19376530942	Vancouver
Williams Lake	O19376505602	Williams Lake
Acsenda School of Management	O19278931852	Vancouver
Adler University	O19394452198	Vancouver
Ajna Yoga Teacher Training	O246351578557	Victoria
Alexander College	O19347185182	Burnaby
All Body Laser Corp	O19394940220	Port Coquitlam
Arbutus College	O19219834012	Vancouver
Art Institute of Vancouver	O19275426742	Vancouver
Ashton College	O19219876582	Vancouver

This is the official website. If you wish to find more schools all around Canada, go to http://www.cic.gc.ca/english/study/study-institutions-list.asp or contact us at www.canadaimmigrate.ca. You can email me directly at lindas@canadaimmigrate.ca, so I can provide you the service to find the best college or university that adjusts to your needs and budget. This can save you a lot of stress and time to get into the institutions.

Authenticate an applicant's foreign credential and determine the equivalent completed Canadian credential.

The purpose of the reports is to award immigration selection points or make program eligibility decisions.

CIC has designated both multipurpose assessment organizations and professional bodies to assess foreign credentials. Multipurpose assessment organizations authenticate and assess foreign educational credentials across a wide range of regulated and non-regulated occupations. The designated organizations are:

- World Education Services (WES),
- International Credential Assessment Service of Canada (ICAS),
- Comparative Education Service (CES), University of Toronto,
- International Qualifications Assessment Service, and
- International Credential Evaluation Service.

Professional bodies authenticate and assess foreign educational credentials to determine how they compare to a Canadian credential needed to practice in their respective regulated occupations. They are also recognized as a step in the licensing process. The designated professional bodies are:

- Medical Council of Canada (MCC); and
- Pharmacy Examining Board of Canada (PEBC).

This will help you to provide your evaluation of your education from abroad. You can either use it to be accepted at a university for a Master Degree or PhD in Canada or to gain points in the program for skilled workers via Express entry.

SOCIAL INSURANCE NUMBER

What is it and where do I obtain it?

The Social Insurance Number (SIN) is a nine-digit number that you need to work in Canada or to have access to government programs and benefits. I would suggest you apply for your SIN number as soon as you obtain a valid work permit, student permit or temporary resident status. A temporary resident permit will allow you to work if it is issued for one year or more. Also, you will need to change your SIN number once you become a Permanent Resident. Please remember to change it as soon as you change your status.

For more information, you can access to www.servicecanada. gc.ca.

DO INTERNATIONAL STUDENT NEED A SOCIAL INSURANCE NUMBER?

International students in Canada may work on or off campus without a work permit if they meet the eligibility requirements of IRCC. Students are required by law to provide their Social Insurance Number (SIN) within three (3) days after the day on which their employment begins. Therefore, it is critical that they have a SIN. For information about obtaining it, access www.servicecanada.gc.ca.

For more information about working while studying in Canada, visit the CIC website or call the CIC Call Centre at 1-888-242-2100.

SETTLEMENT PROGRAM AND RESETTLEMENT ASSISTANCE PROGRAM (RAP)

The Settlement Program assists immigrants and refugees to overcome barriers specific to the newcomer experience (such as a lack of official language skills and limited knowledge of Canada), so that they can participate in the social, cultural, civic and economic life in Canada.

The program focuses on four areas: information and orientation; language training and skills development; labour market access; and welcoming communities. Most services are designed and delivered by service provider organizations, but certain services (such as some information provision) are delivered directly by Immigration, Refugees and Citizenship Canada (IRCC), and some services are delivered overseas. The Refugee Resettlement Assistance Program provides immediate and essential support services and income support to assist in meeting refugees' resettlement needs. Essential services are supported through contributions to service provider organizations. RAP services include, but are not limited to, reception services, assistance with accommodations, links to mandatory federal and provincial programs, life skills training, and orientation on financial and non-financial information.

ABOUT THE AUTHOR

LINDA SALAS WAS BORN AND raised in the town of San Juan del Rio, Queretaro, in Mexico. She is the second of five siblings. Her life as an entrepreneur began when she was very young. She was always selling something; either on the streets of her town or at school. She completed her Law Degree at the University of Queretaro. She first travelled to Europe after completing her degree. She travelled around different parts of Europe, but it was the city of Paris that made Linda aware that she needed to move from Mexico. She wanted what the people of Paris had. They seemed very happy riding their bikes instead of driving, they had time to sit and contemplate the day and drink a coffee, and it seemed part of their culture to read everywhere they went. Linda went back to Mexico and created a clear and determinate plan of when and where she would depart to Canada. Even though some people disagreed with her plans, she decided to listen her intuition and keep moving into the unknown. She made the move to her new country and faced many struggles, but she made it happen because she saw any struggle as an opportunity to continue growing, and she did.

She worked for 8 years with a Law Corporation where she was the manager in charge of the Immigration department. Linda helped thousands of immigrants to get their temporary or permanent resident papers and settle in Canada with the supervision of Michael Golden and Max Wolpert, two great lawyers and mentors.

She then stepped into her dream and opened her own practice that has become very successful. She is the owner of LSF Immigration Consulting. Through this, she has helped hundreds and hundreds of immigrants to become successful. Businesses of all kinds look for Linda's "Midas touch" to transform their business. People look for her advice on immigrating and settling in Canada. She is a great mentor and coach, because she herself is a successful immigrant and business person.

Linda Salas is available to deliver keynote presentations to appropriate audiences. For rates and availability, please contact the author directly at: Lindas@canadaimmigrate.ca or www.canadaimmigrate.ca or www.successfulimmigrantstoday.com.

To order more books, please visit:

www.amazon.com.

Finally, if you have been inspired by this book, the best thing you could ever do is pass that on and be a wonderful role model for others. This world needs more shining lights.

Linda Salas has achieved remarkable success in her life – and she is in her mid-30s.

It does not matter where you are from, regardless of your religion, culture, or beliefs, this book will be a definite help for you to step out of your comfort zone and land into a life of abundance where happiness, wealth, and health will be at its maximum. You will be the protagonist of your own movie, stepping into your purpose in this life and fulfilling your mission.

With all my love and sending light into your path, so that you can grow into consciousness and become aware of your life and how you would like your life be.

Prices: US $20.00 Canadian $24.00 £10 €10 and $250.00 Pesos

Second Printing Second Edition.

66923319R00060